james hull miller's

SELF–SUPPORTING SCENERY

5th Edition Completely Revised

MERIWETHER PUBLISHING LTD.
Colorado Springs, Colorado

Meriwether Publishing Ltd., Publisher
Box 7710
Colorado Springs, CO 80933

ISBN #: 0-916260-91-7
© Copyright MCMLXXI, MCMLXXIII, MCMLXXVI James Hull Miller
© Copyright MCMLXXXII Meriwether Publishing Ltd.
Printed in the United States of America
Fifth Edition
Library of Congress #81-84402

TABLE OF CONTENTS

PREFACE

A typical box set of "flats"

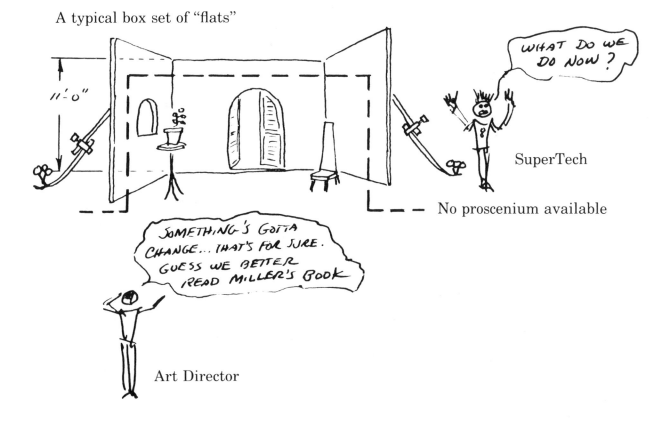

I began working in the theatre in 1934, using traditional proscenium stagecraft, but over the years I found myself spending more and more time assisting those who had neither ample funds for scenery of that sort nor access to conventional stagehouses. By 1958 I had become so totally involved in space staging that I set up the Arts Lab in Shreveport, Louisiana, for research and training in the art and craft of self-supporting scenery.

It should be borne in mind that the scenic solutions presented in this book are not evolved from standard proscenium stagecraft nor are they necessarily compatible with it. Rather, the solutions form a complete way of life on the open stage, and, in pursuing them, one should not look back over one's shoulder for help, but practice the new stagecraft all the more diligently. As it is said, "Form follows function."

A space stage solution for this setting will be found on page 5.

STAGECRAFT I

Wood Fiber Screens

MINESTRONE, PLEASE

Where better to begin than in a class-room, with a very simple piece of scenery. The folding screen shown by the sketch and diagram does four things simultaneously:

1. It masks the doorway,

2. It increases the entrances,

3. It provides a modicum of "Off-stage" shelter, and

4. It makes a background surface for stage decoration.

When the play is over, the screen can be folded up and stored in the classroom closet or loaned out to the art class for a hall display.

A Very Elementary Situation

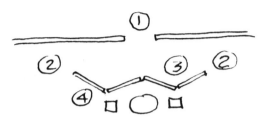

The screen will not be fully effective if there are open cracks at the panel joints. Such cracks are created if metal hinges are used. Yet, masking such cracks will decrease the number of ways the screen may be arranged. Worse yet, lashing the panels together in the manner of "flats" adds the necessity of some sort of bracing which, in turn, interferes with movement behind. The screen will be most flexible if the hinging method permits the panels to be folded either way. For these reasons, the Oriental cloth (or paper) reversible flap hinging system is the only practical solution.

The Reversible Flap Hinge

Before embarking on a full-size folding screen, let's practice the hinging technique on a small model, using cardboard and Kraft paper in place of the usual wood framework with fabric attached. This will allow young people to participate and later make some small folding screens from shipping cartons. However, bear in mind that full-scale scenery from wood fiber products is never practical in the long run.

Cut four pieces of corrugated cardboard 2¾" by 7¼". From a brown paper grocery sack, cut nine strips, each 1" by 7¼". With rubber cement or white glue, and six of the strips, bind the edges of the cardboard

panels which will meet for hinging. These are called "edging" or "masking" strips.

Cut about ⅛" from the lengths of each of the remaining three strips, then cut each of these strips into four pieces of approximately equal size. Do not interchange the pieces from one strip to another! These will be the "hinges." Place two of the panels side by side, and commence attaching the hinges alternately, as shown in the diagram on page 3, being careful that the pieces do not touch one another. Then gently separate the panels to be sure that each hinge piece is attached only to the correct panel.

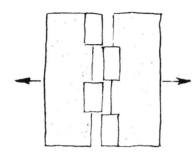

When the glue is dry, turn the panels over. Place a pair of them, just touching, in an inverted "V" position, then slowly lay them down flat in such a way that the free

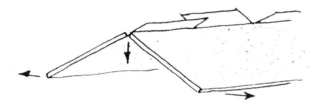

ends of the hinge flaps come up through the joint. All that remains to be done is to glue each flap down to the panel to which it is as yet unattached, while holding the panels firmly and evenly together. Panels thus secured can be folded in either direction. Continue this process until the "fourfold" is complete.

A Working Model

You now have a little working model about one-twelfth the actual size of a typical folding screen suitable for adult use. A designer would say, "A model to the scale of one inch to the foot." The model can be painted, even with a different color on the reverse side, if some care is taken at the hinge joints. If the model is to be finished with colored construction paper, then use the same paper for the edging strips and hinge flaps to begin with, and all the parts of the folding screen will present a uniform appearance regardless of which way a joint is turned! From any reasonable distance

the joint will go unnoticed. Since the joint is a perfect continuity of parts, there is nothing to distract the eye. In this book, scenery joined in this manner will be referred to as "flat-folding."

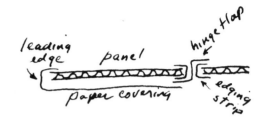

An exaggerated sectional diagram shows the masking or edging strips, a hinge flap, and the panel covering paper. Note how the covering paper also masks the "leading" edge of the screen. Note also that the covering paper does not quite extend to the joint edge so as not to interfere with the reversible flap action of the hinge. If no covering paper is used, then the leading edge should be masked in the same way the joint edges were masked.

Stage Movement Exercises

Directors will find several sets of these model screens very useful in plotting scenery positions. Here, screens with four panels are shown because they are the most practical, especially from the standpoint of stability and handling.

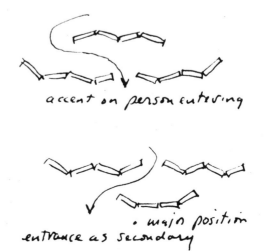

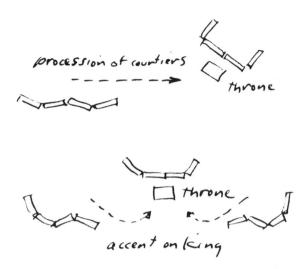

Working Screens of Wood Fiber Products

Many small but useful folding screens can be made from corrugated cardboard taken from bicycle, furniture and appliance crates. Larger panels can be made by gluing together two or more layers of corrugated if the pieces are properly overlapped for structural rigidity. Triple construction corrugated cardboard is also available, as well as light-weight Kraft panels with exceptionally strong honeycomb cores. For further information see Fiber Wallboards on page 11. Obviously the manufacturers of wood fiber products would have us believe that these panels are the ideal solution for all scenery, yet I have not found this to be true except for certain controlled situations such as in television studios and on local stages where scenery is custom-designed for one-shot deals and immediately salvaged or destroyed afterwards.

On the positive side of wood fiber products, with the scenery kept small and doorways or other openings not too large, young people can participate in construction and the elementary school classroom can become a workshop of "cardboard carpentry" so popular with art educators nowadays.

On the negative side, easy participation can be a mixed blessing if sloppy workman-ship results, or, worse still, if such work-manship is taken for granted. Furthermore, children have little respect for and do not take good care of items that are easily damaged, and cardboard scenery is indeed vulnerable. Also, professional artists disagree with "soft options" in place of disciplined training. Furthermore, the cost is about double that of lightly framed cloth panels.

Then there are the limitations of cardboard carpentry which can become most frustrating. Take, for example, the small "sentry-box" sketched below. The pyramidal roof unit can be effectively made of refrigerator carton stock. The opaque walls of the sentry box are easily made of one-inch Celadyn FeatherPANELS, and the archway panel possibly, if a sentry-box is all that is desired of this unit. But consider the panels as parts of a fourfold reversible screen, and the need for a wooden framework for the archway panel, complete with still strip,

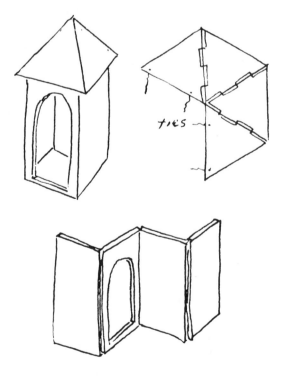

becomes quite obvious, not to mention the temporary joining of the fourfold into the sentry-box configuration, or the attachment of myriad accessories to the archway.

A Box Set Redesigned

On the preceding page a case was made for compact and durable scenery and the good materials and craftsmanship necessary for it. But scenery which is used for space staging has other requirements which place even greater demands on both stagecraft and design. Returning to the sketch on page 1, the removal of the frame exposes the sides of the set, suggesting that the set be made entirely self-supporting and that frames so exposed be covered on both sides. Furthermore, the set is going to be in profile, whereas before one did not necessarily see the top and ends of it.

A solution which satisfies all of the above requirements is sketched out below.

Technically, a twofold screen has been attached to a slab wall in "T" position for self-support, and both the slab and end screen panel have been double-covered to satisfy sightlines. These are matters of mechanics and are easily taught. Design-wise, profile dictates a balance of parts, something not mechanical and often difficult to learn.

The big problem with most scenery for space staging is that it can't be copied over from real life, there being no convenient picture frame to terminate the copy. So what you take from life has to be reworked into some sort of form that artistically "stops by itself" in space. Hence, the overall profile assumes tremendous importance. This matter is discussed in considerable depth in the section on scene design. Our concern here is with the mechanical aspects, which, in turn, will dictate the materials and shop equipment necessary for this kind of stagecraft.

The simpler construction is that of the slab, which is built up of battens which measure ¾" by about 1¾" and which are framed on edge rather than flat. In effect, we have a miniaturization of house wall construction with its "2x4" studs.

A one-inch vertical slot at the middle of the slab is framed by two battens turned at right angles to the on-edge construction. These are called "clamping strips."

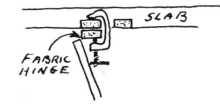

The enlarged diagram shows a folding strip (which has been cloth-flap hinged to the archway screen panel) clamped to one of the two slab clamping strips. (The shaft of a standard two-inch C-clamp has been shortened.)

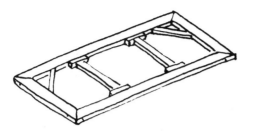

Of the two systems — flat-folding and clamped-slab — the folding screen is the more complex in construction since the frames must be uniformly ¾" thick and therefore without the customary strapping over the joints. With this setting, the end panel must be covered on both sides. However, if the archway panel is also double-covered, the setting can be turned around to represent an outdoor scene as well. In this case, the hinged batten strip is reversed and secured to the other slot batten in the slab.

The cover picture illustrates a more usual clamp-together situation, where both the window wall and the garden archway wall are of similar slab construction, one being clamped directly to the other.

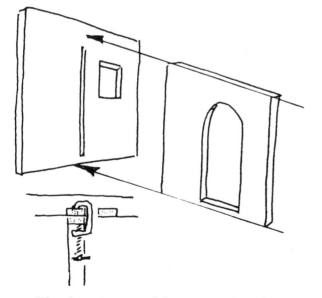

The drawings and diagrams thus far are by no means technically complete, but rather they are intended to point up the several working concepts for making scenery freestanding and self-supporting. These matters will be taken up in great detail later on.

When you consider the structural demands of this sort of scenery — doorway sills, shutter mountings, internal framing in slabs for connections, and a host of other attachments — and then add portability, compactness for storage, etc., it should be quite obvious that corrugated cardboard and other wood fiber products, no matter how thick, have little application here, save for trims, etc.

Therefore, the remainder of the Stagecraft I section will be devoted to setting up a shop, procuring the necessary materials, and mastering the various structuring and covering procedures required to get the unit on page 5 built. This will open the way for a design discussion; following that, Stagecraft II will pick up where Stagecraft I stops.

Setting Up the Shop
Useful Hand Tools

18" x 14" FRAMING SQUARE, for trueing up platform frame construction

TRY SQUARE (if try square has a level, eliminate level listed below)

PROTRACTOR, essential for determining angles for transfer to miter gauge and for many other calculations

Small LEVEL, used with protractor to figure balance angles, cantenary construction, etc.

PLUMB BOB, used with protractor and level for certain curved construction

6' WOOD FOLDING RULE, more useful than steel tapes for measuring

DIAGONAL PLIERS, especially useful for extracting light box resin-coated nails

LONG-NOSE PLIERS, especially useful for extracting staples

Bostitch STAPLE REMOVER G7B, not as effective as long-nose pliers, but very useful

Stanley UTILITY KNIFE No. 299

MILL BASTARD FILE, for smoothing tips of nails which do not penetrate far enough to be bent over

RUBBER MALLET, for resetting lids on paint cans

2" SPRING CLAMPS, Stanley No. 43-162, half dozen, where C-clamps will not fit

MITER BOX with back saw, for accurate miter cuts in place of table saw; captive saw type recommended

C-CLAMPS, 2" standard throat, such as Stanley No. H152 or Adjustable No. 1420, for joining units constructed by the "on-edge" principle; about five dozen recommended for active groups

SHEARS, for cutting cloth

Specialized Hand Tools

No. B13 True Temper recommended

Most people think the right hammer is just any hammer. In truth, devices for pounding are as specialized as golf clubs. Avoid hammers whose heads are highly chamfered because it will be difficult to strike the nails at the corner miter joints when flat-framing on floor or work bench.

Avoid the straight claw or "ripping" hammer, as the balance of the round claw hammer is better. The use for which a straight claw hammer is designed is not found in our stagecraft system. And there is no need for hammers heavier than 13 ounces.

Staple Tacker

U.S. — Use Swingline 101 and Arrow JT-21 tackers with 5⁄16" staples; not Swingline 101-HD as staple gauge is too heavy.

Britain — Use No. 330 Velos Lightning Tacker with ¼" (6mm) staples and Rexel Triumph Tacker MK2 Model 200 with 5⁄16" (8mm) staples.

In selecting other tackers, do not exceed staple gauges used for above. Also check handle action for easy operation. When using strong burlap colors, rub staple sticks with magic marker matching color before inserting staples in tacker.

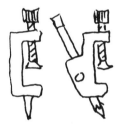
Stanley Trammel Points No. 4TP

Essential for arch construction. Otherwise, fashion a giant compass in the shop.

Giant Compass

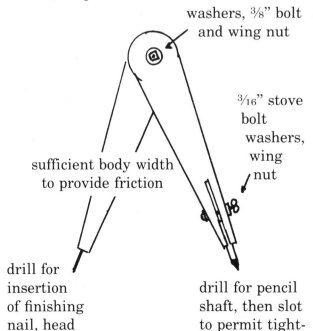

washers, 3⁄8" bolt and wing nut

3⁄16" stove bolt washers, wing nut

sufficient body width to provide friction

drill for insertion of finishing nail, head removed

drill for pencil shaft, then slot to permit tightening

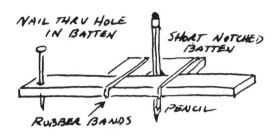

Emergency Compass

Parallel Rule

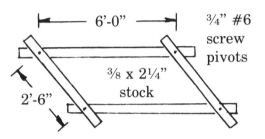

Make this yourself in the shop. It is invaluable for determining the lay of arch braces, for calculating widths for flat-framing arch sweep stock, and for the layout of patterns for arch sweeps for the on-edge framing for clamped scenery.

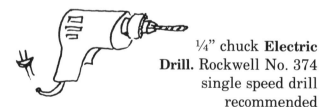

¼" chuck **Electric Drill.** Rockwell No. 374 single speed drill recommended

The electric drill with the ³⁄₃₂" bit is used continually to make nail passage holes in the first member of a corner miter joint and in arch sweeps for the flat framing techniques.

Other useful spiral bits include the following ⁵⁄₆₄", ⁷⁄₆₄", ³⁄₁₆" and ¼". Also the ½" countersink bit. Speedbor wood bits as follows: ¼", ⁵⁄₁₆", ³⁄₈", ½", ⁵⁄₈", ¾" and 1" for work in conjunction with wood dowels, and with these bits, of course, an industrial quality drill is essential. The additional $15 or so is well spent in the long run.

Portable Electric Sabre Saw

Useful for cutting clamping slots in plywood platform tops and for other rough work, but certainly a poor substitute for the band or jig saw machines, or even hand tools, because of excessive vibration and crudeness of blade.

K-11 Cutawl

This unique hand power tool is the handmaiden of the store window display industry. The Cutawl will perform with superb efficiency and with greater accuracy the tasks of the jig, sabre, keyhole and scroll saws. It is especially useful in large-scale panel perforations with laminated cardboards such as Upson Board. Send for literature: Cutawl Co., Bethel, Connecticut 06801.

Larger Machinery

Table Saw

Rockwell Delta 9" Circular Tilting Arbor Bench Saw. Catalog No. 50-810 includes rip fence, guide bars, extension wings, miter gauge, blade, motor and open stand as shown on page 8. A good table saw is a necessity for this stagecraft system. And this is one place where quality must not be compromised. Do not substitute a radial arm (pullover) saw.

Spray Gun

An optional item. Useful for shading. Amateurs achieve fine effects using stencils. See the section on painting.

Rockwell Delta 14" Wood Cutting Band Saw No. 28-297, with 62-680 heavy duty ½ hp single phase motor and 1334 switch rod. Use ½" saw blade.

Substitutes for this important tool are time-consuming and less accurate.

Sturdy Work Table

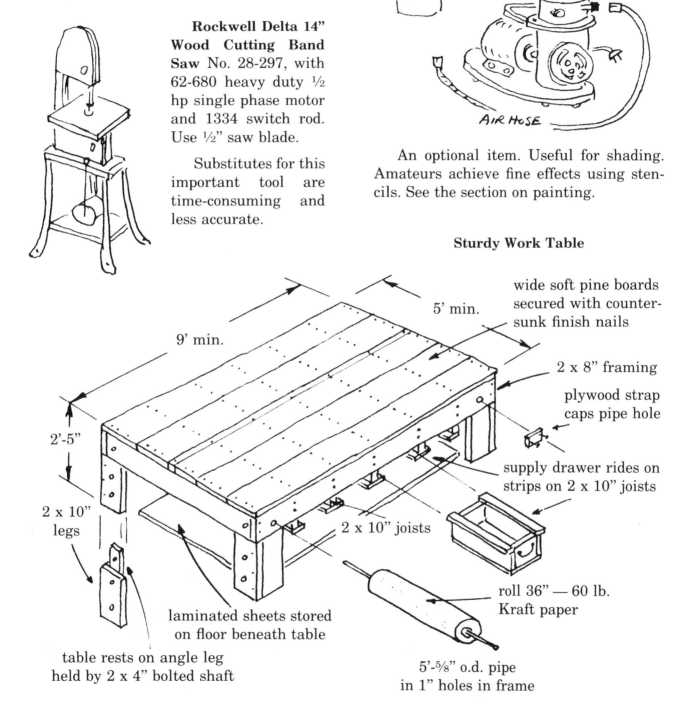

wide soft pine boards secured with counter-sunk finish nails

5' min.

9' min.

2 x 8" framing

plywood strap caps pipe hole

2'-5"

supply drawer rides on strips on 2 x 10" joists

2 x 10" legs

2 x 10" joists

roll 36" — 60 lb. Kraft paper

laminated sheets stored on floor beneath table

table rests on angle leg held by 2 x 4" bolted shaft

5'-⅝" o.d. pipe in 1" holes in frame

The work table is not to be confused with a work bench. The work table is for layout while framing, joining and covering screens, and the height is correct for these operations. Allow a minimum of 1½' walkway completely around the table. The soft pine top is for temporary nailing to secure frames while fitting and to receive the ends of nails during the construction of lap-jointed step and platform frames. Countersunk nails permit the use of utility knives without fouling their cutting edges.

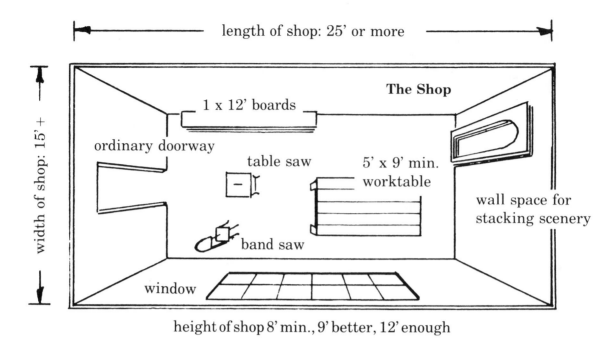

length of shop: 25' or more

width of shop: 15' +

The Shop

1 x 12' boards

ordinary doorway

table saw

5' x 9' min.
worktable

band saw

wall space for
stacking scenery

window

height of shop 8' min., 9' better, 12' enough

The Shop

One of the rationales for this stagecraft is that the scenery can pass through ordinary doorways and stand up in just about any place. Therefore, in a pinch, the shop can be quite small and yet be serviceable. Most doorways provide a clearance of 2'-7½" x 6'-7½", which will pass a slab unit diagonally whose lesser dimension is 6'-9".

The band and table saws should not be fastened down so they can be maneuvered for large pieces. Note the relative positions of the open doorway, the table saw and the work table, for ripping long boards. On the other hand, never raise the operating heights of the power saws through the use of castered platforms. If you do not wish to slide them around, purchase the retractable casters made especially for these tools. There should be at least two 20-amp circuits in the shop just for the convenience outlets for tools. Locate these outlets near the baseboard. If a tool cabinet is built, it should be narrow and be castered. Having lots of daylight as well as artificial illumination adds a safety factor. Tungsten lamps are always

preferable to fluorescent tubes. Sixty foot candles are recommended at table height. The shop floor must not be slick. Remove all waxes on concrete or wood. A glossy shop floor plus sawdust can be extremely dangerous, especially where power tools are employed. With a good industrial vacuum cleaner carpet without padding can be used.

Materials and Supplies

Lumber. Use ¾" white or ponderosa pine or spruce for framing. The basic framing member for this system is a batten ¾" thick and 1¾" to 1⅞" wide, though it will be necessary to standardize for slab construction. I use 1¹³⁄₁₆" and strongly recommend it. "1x2s" are too light for flat-framing and not wide enough for slab construction. "1x3s" are wider than needed for flat-framing, and they make the slabs too bulky. Many other special widths will be required also, so if you don't have a table saw I would advise not proceeding further. On the other hand, to be able to rip up wood to specification means that with careful sawing you can use cheap grades. I use No. 3 Common myself. But avoid boards having hard veins and knots lying sideways (spikes), since both are prone to warp when ripped. In England, use the standard 2" x 1" (50 x 25mm) planed deal for basic framing. Stock strips of ⅞" x ⅞" are also useful if no power saw is available.

Plywood. Use ¾" for ramps and platform tops. Flatness is more important than blemishes. Use ¼" for arch sweeps, for slab construction and for complex sandwiches such as shutters. Use ⅜" for the simpler sandwich construction, for round-topped doors, etc. With ¼" and ⅜", purchase the best grades only.

Fiber Wallboards (laminated cardboard). The best known of these in the theatre trade are the Beaverboard and Upson Board panels, usually in 4' x 8' sheets, which can be bent upon curved forms and which are also easily perforated for panel designs. Of these, Upson is the more durable product, and the ³⁄₁₆" thickness is the best for most tasks. It can be bent into curves as minimal as a 2' radius for tower walls, etc. It is ideal material for the complex profile work and intricate patterns processed by the Cutawl machine for the display trade. Upson has a thinner and more flexible panel called E-Z Curve (⅛"), but this punctures easily. Their thicker ¼" panel is used for display where there is no underlying structural framework. The popularity of gypsum and other products for lightweight partitions in the building trade has made these fiber boards difficult to obtain.

Prefinished panels, see page 112.

Hollow Core Panelboards. "Tri-Wall" is similar to cardboard carton stock except that it has a triple lamination of corrugated, is just over ½" thick, and is exceptionally strong. Write: Workshop for Learning Things, 5 Bridge St., Watertown, MA 02172.

"Celadyn" is the trade name for a honeycomb core Kraft sheet which is available in a variety of thicknesses, the most useful for theatre people being the 1" 4x8' Featherpanel. Write: Bell Fibre Products Corp., P.O. Box 264, Michigan City, IN 46360.

Nails. Nails should be resin-coated and of the "light box" gauge. They are often called "cement-coated" nails. When these nails are driven, the resin glue heats and bonds the nail to the wood, thus doubling the holding power over "bright" nails. The 6 and 8 penny sizes are the most frequently used and can be had in 50-pound cardboard containers. Some 3 penny cement-coated nails are also required, but these should be purchased a few pounds at a time. In England, resin-coated nails are not available. 3, 2½ and 2" ovals will have to do. Some 1" wire nails will also be needed.

Staples (see STAPLE TACKERS, in tool section). The Swingline 101-5 is the correct staple. Arrow makes a similar staple for their JT-21, but the latter tacker is more fatiguing, and the staples are not interchangeable. Allow 3500 per double-covered fourfold screen set. A staple must be long enough to pass through several layers of fabric, usually burlap, and still be secure. Yet it must be easily removable when fabrics are restretched or replaced. And the gauge must be light enough to cause the staple to be camouflaged in the texture of the fabric. This does not leave much of a choice!

Fabrics for Covering Frames

Burlap (British "hessian"). Burlap makes an ideal covering material for several reasons. It comes in a wide range of dyed colors. Its texture has a quality look, even in daylight. The texture camouflages the staples which secure the burlap to the frames. The texture also camouflages the small slits and holes that are used for the attachment of decor and other scenic units. 9 or 10 ounce is the correct weight. You may find some dyed burlap at your mill ends discount store, though it is considerably more economical to purchase it in wholesale lots. If your local dry goods wholesaler cannot obtain it for you, write the Sea-Rich Corp., 2512 South Damen Ave., Chicago, IL 60608, for their Decorator Burlap Color Card and price quotations for the 35/36" width. The 25-yard roll is a standard unit. While widths may vary somewhat elsewhere, it is inadvisable to purchase much wider stock since the average folding screen panel seldom exceeds three feet and wider pieces can be sewn when needed or, better still, joined by stapling to common battens.

I have found the following Sea-Rich colors to be the most satisfactory in the long run, taking into consideration resistance to fading, richness of hue, general appearance under most lighting conditions, etc. Often it is wiser to alter one's design in order to take advantage of fabrics which are inherently good-looking on the stage rather than be blindly faithful to some *a priori* conception.

53	Alaska Gold	106	Pencil Yellow
68	Barn Red	108	Taffy Brown
74	Bean Pot Brown	114	Purple
75	Cobbler Brown	116	Chartreuse
76	Natural	124	Eggshell
79	Leaf Green	142	Spring Blue
	143	Emerald Green	

Shipping from Sea-Rich: United Parcel Service handles 100 pounds per day per destination (50-pound limit per bundle). This will permit an order of six 25-yard rolls. There is no minimum charge. With truck freight, the minimum charge is for 100 pounds, and for this, seven rolls can be shipped.

In England, a good 10-ounce natural hessian can be obtained from upholstery sources. The 7½-ounce hessian is too loosely woven. There is a tightly woven hessian milled in Scotland, often called "Dundee," which is sold as a substitute for scene canvas (Brodie & Middleton, 79 Long Acre, London WC2). This has poor texture and is unpleasantly glossy, but it is readily available and is stocked in school supply. Dyed hessian of good quality is available from Russel & Chappel, 23 Monmouth St., London WC2; Boyle & Son, Ltd., Clayton Wood Close West Park Ring Road, Leeds; MacCulloch & Wallis, Ltd., 25/6 Dering St., London W1. Widths and intensity of color vary.

CAUTION: Dyed burlaps should be kept from direct exposure to sunlight and, when stored, should be protected from strong light and heat, as the color will fade. Refresh faded burlap by saturating the fibers with ordinary household dyes, such as Rit. Recolor faded burlap by spray painting only, preferably with thinned oils.

Unbleached Muslin. For those who wish to paint completely over a sized surface in the traditional manner, muslin will be required. However, glueing must be substituted for stapling, which makes fabric hinge construction for folding scenery more difficult and time consuming. However, some muslin should be kept on hand for the occasional flap-hinging of wood units such as shutters and profiled arches, and for "cardboard" scenery and such.

Denim is woven of a mixture of threads already dyed, thus giving it some texture and opposite faces of dissimilar shades. For the sake of variety, purchase locally by the yard as required.

Indian Head offers an excellent color selection and is also a serviceable material. Texture is minimal but OK.

NOTE: Since the above fabrics are somewhat transparent, lining (undersurfacing) is necessary. An inexpensive solution is the use of two layers of 60-pound or heavier Kraft paper. The 36" roll is recommended. Purchase this from your local paper wholesale house. The same paper will also be used for patterns for both slab-type arch sweeps and round-topped door parts. In England, heavy Kraft paper is hard to come by, and a substitute can be made by laminating four layers of newsprint by means of wheat paste.

Supplies such as paints, chalks and brushes will be covered in the section on Scene Painting. Materials for colored shadow projection will be listed in the Architectural section. And see page 94 for sources for color filters for the latter and for spotlights for stage lighting.

Flameproofing

Wood, cloth and paper are porous by nature and are therefore capable of absorbing flameproofing and fire retardant solutions. Most scenic supply houses carry flameproofing crystals which can be dissolved in water and applied to the surfaces in question, usually by spray. In the U.S., Paramount Theatrical Supplies, 32 W. 20th St., New York, NY 10011, or Olesen Co., 1535 Ivar Ave., Hollywood, CA 90028. In England, Brodie & Middleton, 79 Long Acre, London WC2. Many fabrics can be had already flameproofed or can be flameproofed upon request. However, it should be kept in mind that the chemical solutions in fire retardants deteriorate fabrics, especially burlap, so one should use retardants only when absolutely necessary. The need for retardants is obvious in proscenium theatre stagehouses with the many curtains, backdrops and large settings, but a folding screen or two on a platform stage is quite another matter, the screens being, in effect, an ex-

tension of the furniture. Also, burlap that is securely stapled down over Kraft paper does not support combustion, as can be seen by holding a lighted match against a finished screen panel.

Using Power Tools

Checking the Table Saw

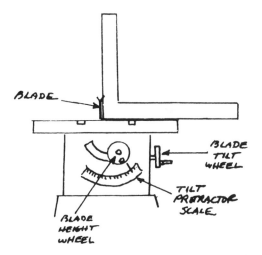

First check the accuracy of the blade tilt protractor scale by raising the blade to its maximum exposed height and using a framing square, avoiding, of course, contact with the set of a tooth. The indicator should be at 0°. Some saws have a positive limit stop adjustment when the blade is perpendicular to the table top.

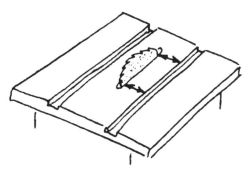

Next measure from the extreme ends of the exposed blade as it intersects the table to one of the grooves. If these measurements are not equal, then the table top and blade assembly must be realigned. If you do not have the instruction booklet, refer to the Delta manual titled "Getting the Most Out of Your Circular Saw and Jointer."

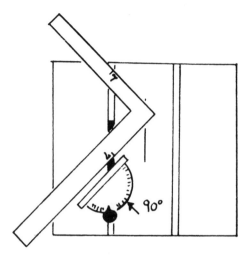

Next check the cross-cut miter gauge. In the sketch above, the framing square is aligned with the groove for a 45° angle. Loosen the holding knob on the gauge and slide the gauge up against the square. Then see if the angle indicator and the automatic stop are in adjustment.

Note the arrow pointing to the center of the miter gauge scale. The scale should read 90° here, not 0°. I mention this because I once found a piece of equipment so mismarked, thus rendering inaccurate all degree specifications in the manual which involved the use of the miter gauge. If this situation should apply, subtract the specified angle from 90° to compensate.

Next examine the sides of the V-groove pulleys on both motor and arbor shafts for any flaws or warps. Also check the V-belt itself for tears. Faults here produce undue vibrations which, in excess, cause a thumping sound. A slight ticking noise, especially when the saw has been turned off and the blade is slowing down, indicates a loosening set screw on either pulley.

Ripping a Batten

Move the rip fence into position measuring between the blade and the fence for the desired batten width. Set the height of the blade about ½" above the thickness of the board.

Provide a surface almost as high as the saw table for the board to slide onto after it has passed over the table. By having this support, one person can handle the entire ripping operation with far more accuracy than with a helper.

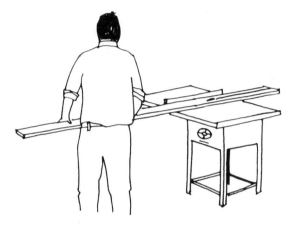

Turn on the saw. Now pick up the board at the balance. Lay one end just over the edge of the saw table. Shift the hands back a few feet. Note the position of the arms in the sketch. This sketch shows a left-handed person. Reverse for a right-handed one. The body should be on the side of the board opposite to the rip guide and turned to a 45° angle. The hand on the edge of the board away from the guide is forward, while the hand on the other edge is to the rear. Note the excellent degree of control one has of the board! It must always ride evenly against the rip guide.

Advance, pushing the board into the blade. Move the feet in crab-like fashion, one over the other, to prevent body sway. Keep moving the hands back. When the end of the board reaches the table, pick up a scrap stick of wood and push the board through. Never advance the hands into the blade area when ripping.

If the board tends to "walk away" from the guide, or the reverse, making the rip difficult, you have not got the rip guide properly adjusted. If the blade bends and follows the grain, the blade is dull. If smoke is generated, it is very dull. One should have at least two blades so one can be at the sharpener's. If no such expert is available where you live, purchase the longer-lasting carbide-tipped blades.

Crosscutting

Remove the rip fence. If you are right-handed, place the miter gauge in the left table slot. Hold the batten against the guide with the right hand and support the batten with the left. Sight along the blade and bring the mark on the batten into line with the blade. Remember which piece of the batten you want, for the cut will remove about ⅛". Advance the batten into the saw. When the cut is made, withdraw the guide before releasing the hand. Do not reach for the piece left on the table unless it extends beyond the slot. Rather, knock it off the table with a scrap stick or with the pencil from behind your ear.

Safety Tips

By withdrawing the guide, you won't risk reaching for it later, thus extending your hand toward a saw blade that may still be running.

Always remove any wood left on the table after a cut is completed. A small piece especially is liable to be jostled into the saw through vibration and be thrown toward the operator with incredible velocity.

After sighting for a crosscut, move the head away from the line of the blade in case small knots or other hard particles are encountered which can be thrown out by the saw.

NEVER use the rip fence as a cut-off gauge when cross-cutting. The moment the wood is cut, the saw blade will warp the cut end around slightly, causing it to jam and possibly to be thrown out toward the operator.

When cutting an unknown angle drawn on a batten without the use of the miter gauge, again, have both hands holding the batten on one side of the saw blade.

Adjusting the Band Saw

Before using the band saw, remove both the upper and lower blade guards and retract the blade guides and supports (A and B in the sketch on page 16) both above *and* below the table.

The shaft of the upper wheel is set on a camber device controlled by a knob with locking nut. By loosening this nut, the knob can be turned and the angle of the wheel altered. While turning the upper wheel by hand, adjust this angle so that the blade rides precisely at the center of the wheel tire. Then set the locking nut.

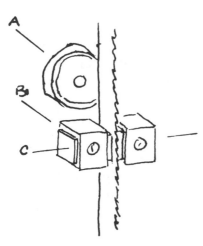

Now check the blade tension scale for proper blade tension. This is calibrated by blade widths. Next, loosen the screws which hold the blade guide blocks (C) and remove these blocks. Check to be sure that the ends which ride alongside the blade are perfectly true. If not, file these faces flat at perfect right angles. The metal is soft, and this should not be difficult. Reinsert the blocks, but leave the set screws loose. Next, while turning the upper wheel, advance the upper blade support wheel (A) until it is just touching the rear edge of the blade and secure it. Repeat this with the lower blade support wheel. Next, advance the blade guide block assembly (B) until the blocks come just short of touching the teeth of the blade. Then, while holding a piece of index card between each guide block and the blade, gently move the guide blocks inward, being careful not to move the blade one way or the other. Tighten the block set screws. Repeat below. Replace the blade guards and you are ready to go! Note: More expensive band saws may have wheels in place of the guide blocks, but the adjustment procedure is much the same.

It is obvious that this entire procedure must be repeated each time you change to a blade of a different width. It is also wise to go through this procedure the first time you use a particular band saw in order to satisfy yourself that it is functioning correctly. Should you use an imperfectly adjusted saw, you will run the risk of blade breakage, not to mention the difficulty of making proper cuts. Further, by going through this procedure you will better understand how the band saw works — and you will be especially careful in withdrawing a piece of wood from a cut that cannot be completed for some reason, for you will know now that nothing is holding the blade on the wheels but its natural tendency to ride up to center if nothing is forcefully pulling it away. When you are making a cut, the blade rides against the blade support wheels, of course, and can't be pushed off in that direction. In this respect, it is particularly important that the blade rides naturally on the wheel tires and that the blade support wheels do not spin around until a cut is begun. There will be times when it will be impossible to withdraw a board easily due to warpage closing the cut. In such a situation, turn off the band saw. Insert wedges in the cut and work the board out by hand. If necessary, remove the upper wheel guard and slowly turn the wheel by hand.

Basic Framing

A Set for a Simple Dwelling

The construction of this little setting, which is the "space stage" version of the proscenium "box" set from page 1, will be used to illustrate basic framing techniques. The only items not covered in this section will be the shutters, which will be explained in Stagecraft II.

Before proceeding with any scenery I always make a little model from index card stock, usually at the scale of ¼" = 1'-0". Include any door or window openings, with doors and shutters operable, if possible. I construct directly from this model, but for the beginner I have made some "working drawings" at the scale of ½" = 1'-0", and I

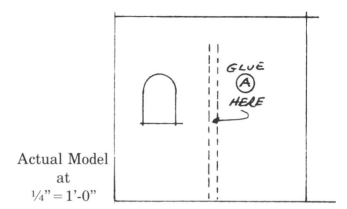

Actual Model at ¼" = 1'-0"

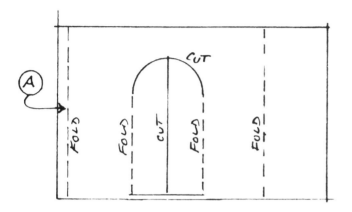

suggest that a little ¼" scale model be made from these dimensions so you can see what I am talking about. The model shows the degree of self-support; the relationship of parts, one to another, both in size and profile; and the proper size and location of any openings for doors, windows, etc. And as you turn the model this way and that, bear in mind that the director just may move the set around during rehearsals, for there is nothing to prevent him, the set being self-supporting and not attached to anything else. In fact this is one of the big attractions of self-supporting scenery.

With the longer twofold butting into the shorter slab, a proper "balance of parts" is best achieved by making the twofold slightly lower than the slab. Also, the window arch should be slightly lower than the doorway arch, otherwise there is that optical illusion which makes the wider of two adjacent openings of equal height appear lower than the narrower. And in the interests of furniture placement, it will be better if the doors themselves open outwards. Since doors do not usually open outward, except in public

places, I have substituted shutters. If the set is turned around for an exterior scene, the shutters, folded back against the wall, will add pictorial interest.

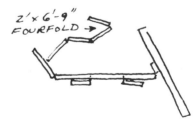

With the set in the latter position, it is at once apparent that a small interior backing screen will be needed. To set the dimensions let us keep two things in mind: the height of an adult and the usefulness of the interior masking screen elsewhere. On page 2 it is suggested that a simple screen be high enough to mask an ordinary doorway. Thus a minimum height is 6'-9". And while

a threefold with 2' panels will suffice for our setting, a fourfold is always more useful, and one panel can be turned back out of the way. A reasonable archway height would be 6', and, allowing 15" above that for a feeling of solidity to the wall, we obtain a total screen height of 7'-3". And the mask-

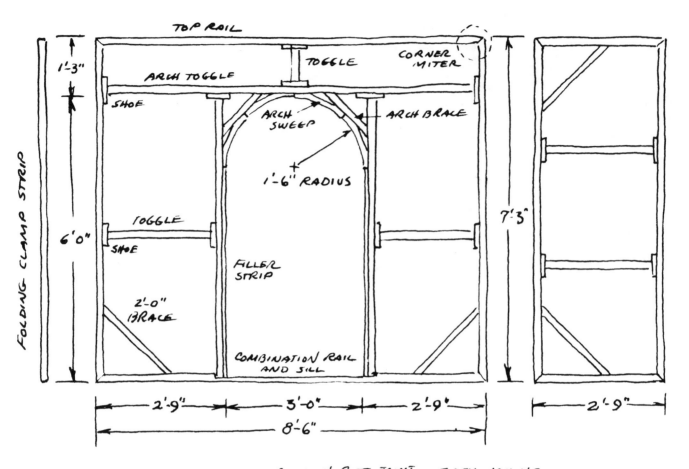

TOP RAIL

TOGGLE

CORNER MITER

ARCH TOGGLE

SHOE

ARCH SWEEP

ARCH BRACE

1'-6" RADIUS

TOGGLE

SHOE

FILLER STRIP

FOLDING CLAMP STRIP

1'-3"

6'-0"

7'-3"

2'-0" BRACE

COMBINATION RAIL AND SILL

2'-9"   3'-0"   2'-9"

8'-6"

2'-9"

ing screen is 9" higher than the archway, but 6" lower than the top of the setting. Note especially these dimensions in contrast to the dimensions of the similar setting in a proscenium environment on page 1. The flats which make up the box setting are 11' high, but this dimension has more to do with the proscenium width and overhead masking than pure aesthetic considerations. Our little space version will appear equally large because it is not as wide and because it is freestanding.

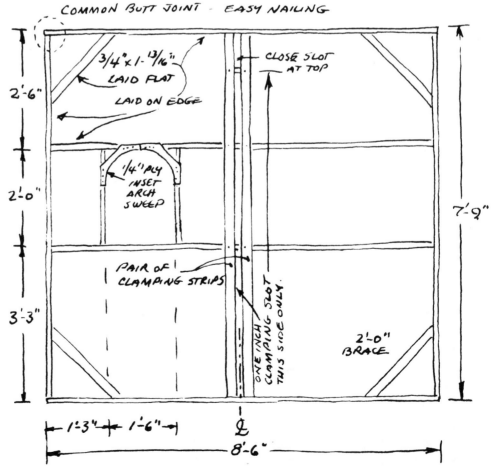

COMMON BUTT JOINT - EASY NAILING

3/4" × 1-13/16" LAID FLAT

LAID ON EDGE

CLOSE SLOT AT TOP

2'-6"

1/4" PLY INSET ARCH SWEEP

2'-0"

PAIR OF CLAMPING STRIPS

3'-3"

ONE INCH CLAMPING SLOT THIS SIDE ONLY.

2'-0" BRACE

7'-9"

1'-3"   1'-6"

8'-6"

Structural Drawings
½" = 1'-0"

"On-Edge" Framing

Since the slab is easier to construct than the "flat-framed" pieces, it will be built first. But you must decide now, and for all time, what the precise width of your ¾" framing stock is going to be; otherwise, you will have trouble keeping slabs perfectly flush on both sides. I recommend the ¹³⁄₁₆" width. On page 5, the simple butt joint for slab construction is illustrated. Use 8 penny cement-coated nails. Assemble the perimeter of the slab and insert the clamping strips at right angles and flush to the rear surface. The lower toggle can be inserted when a notched joint has been prepared in order that the clamping strips and toggle can pass one another.

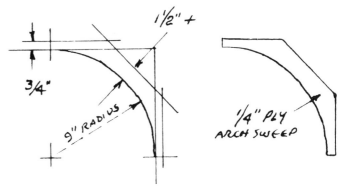

Then, secure the remaining toggle and window stiles, true up the frame, add the braces, flush to one side or the other, then

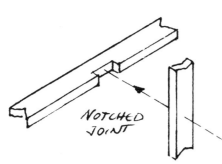

The simplest way to make a notched joint of this sort is to raise the circular saw blade ¾" above the table and rake out the joint. Secure the clamping strips to the lower toggle with 6 penny cement-coated nails. The tips will pass through, so file these flush with a mill bastard file. The upper or arch toggle cannot be seated permanently until both the notches for the clamping strips and the long notches for insetting the arch sweeps are completed.

On a piece of Kraft paper, lay out the arch sweep pattern, then trace this pattern four times on ¼" plywood. Prepare the sweeps with the band saw. After completing the notch for the clamping strips, lay in this toggle and the window stiles and mark for the insets for the seating of the arch sweeps. It will be easier to prepare these long notches with the band saw. (See diagram at lower right.)

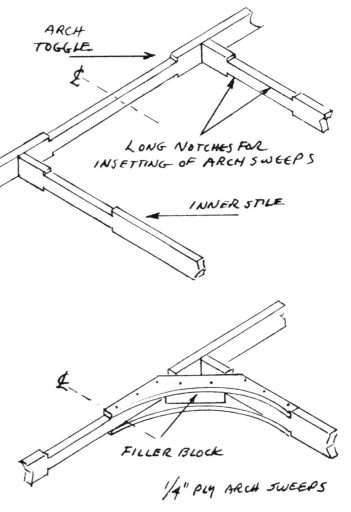

the arch sweeps, with 3 penny cement-coated nails, and finally, the custom-cut filler blocks.

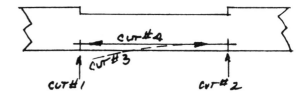

"Flat" Framing

Now we turn to a more difficult type of construction, with "flat" frames uniformly ¾" thick and flush on *both* faces, not only for fully reversible folding, but also because a great deal of scenery in space has to be double-covered to satisfy ordinary sight lines. In this example, the slab obviously has to be double-covered as well, for even folded back rather than forward as shown, the rear face would be visible through the archway. So it will be necessary to build without the customary ¼" ply "patchwork" that is traditionally used to cover the butt joints of the flat-framed scenery of the proscenium theatre.

Before starting construction, rip up a number of boards into the customary 1¹³⁄₁₆" strips and lay aside the best pieces for the longer vertical members. It is unwise to use poor pieces for flat framing since it is difficult to strengthen cracks or repair breaks, whereas with the slab construction, you can patch weak places very easily. Short lengths can be cut between knots, etc. There will be very little waste for, right away, we will need some 8" or 9" pieces for the "shoes." There is no set width for these pieces, from ¾" to ⅞" or thereabouts being satisfactory.

The smaller folding panel will be made first. With the miter gauge set at precisely 45°, cut two pieces at 7'-3" and two pieces at 2'-9". With the electric drill and a ⁷⁄₆₄" bit, make the lead holes as shown in the sketch, offset so that corner cross-nailing is possible.

Make hole
about
1" back

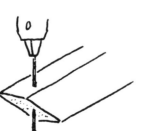

Lay the battens down on a somewhat rough floor to prevent them from slipping around, and complete the corner miters with 8 penny cement-coated nails. Start the nail as shown in the sketch. Once the nail passes through the lead hole and catches onto the holding batten, shift all the body weight to that batten to prevent the joint from opening up.

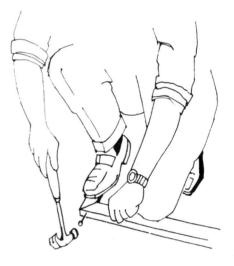

The toggles are inserted next. For this, you will need some "shoes," those little pieces made from scrap about 8" or 9" long and from ¾" to ⅞" wide, or thereabouts. The method of measuring the toggles is shown on the following page.

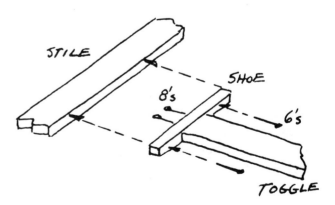

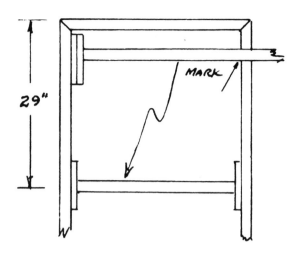

By measuring for the toggles in the manner shown, you don't have to figure actual measurements, so the chance for error is reduced. Nor do you have to cut the shoes a precise width so long as you don't mix up the shoes and toggles. If you are making a series of identical frames, keep one stile and one rail for modules. These cut down on erroneous measurements also.

Before inserting the braces, lay the frame on the work table and nail down one stile temporarily as shown in preparation for "squaring up" the frame. The holding nails should be at the positions indicated, so the braces should be already cut. For these holding nails, use "brights" rather than "cement-coated" so that they can be withdrawn easily.

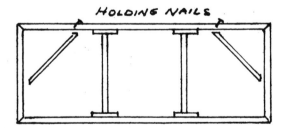

Next measure the frame diagonally in both directions. If these measurements are equal the frame is true and should be secured to the work table by nailing the other stile down, or, better yet, placing holding nails through the rails where the other ends of the braces will terminate. If the diagonals are not equal, then make them so by moving

the other stile in the appropriate direction. For example, if the diagonals are off by ½", then move the stile ¼" in the direction of the shorter reading.

There are certain rules for all braces: (1) a pair of braces per frame are all that is necessary; (2) always place braces against the same stile, if possible; (3) the angle of the brace should be 45°, where possible; (4) the juncture of brace to rail should occur at about the halfway point or slightly beyond; and (5) the brace need not be of full width stock — 1⅝" or even 1½" will do nicely. These braces are 2' long, an OK length for most framing, so some can be cut ahead of time and kept in stock.

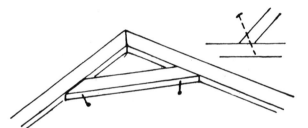

Special care must be taken in securing the braces. The quickest way is to drill lead holes through the brace as shown and set the braces in with 8 penny cement-coated nails. Hammering these nails represents the first blows struck to the frame that are not self-aligning! The holding nails are not sufficient to prevent the frame from being knocked out of kilter, so get up on the table and really put your weight firmly on the stile and rails in turn. I prefer preparing screw holes in the braces and securing them in this manner as shown in the sketch below.

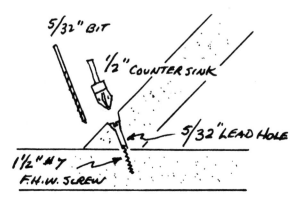

The larger frame requires a specially prepared rail so that the sill part of the archway is not over 1¼" high, which I have determined from experience will satisfy the necessary structural connection without being too high to step over easily. Note particularly that the inner stile is held back ¾" from the assigned opening. The arch toggle will also be held back ¾" from the assigned archway top, so the distance from the top of the frame down to the lower edge of the arch toggle will be 1'-2¼". The best way to secure the inner stile to the combination rail and sill piece is by screwing up through a couple of specially prepared holes, as shown on the diagram. Select a 2" or 3" screw, use a Speedbor bit to pass the screw head in a ways, then the proper bit to prepare a hole through the remainder of the sill to pass the shank.

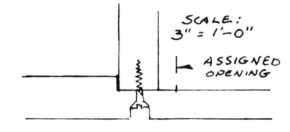

Assemble the frame completely with the exception of the parts for the arch and the filler strips. Secure the frame to the work table after laying down a piece of Kraft paper on the table below the area where the arch is to be constructed. For this operation, we will require the trammel points and a couple of little blocks of wood marked as shown. A yardstick is also helpful. On this first go-around the parallel rule will prove informative, if one has been made similar to that shown on page 8.

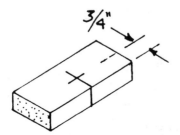

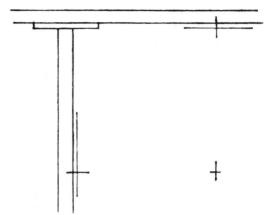

In order to avoid redundancy, only half of the arch construction will be shown. The first diagram shows lines drawn ¾" away from the inner stile and arch toggle. To draw these lines, I use one of the blocks turned on edge as a guide. On these lines the points are located showing the beginning (spring) and center (crown) of the archway. Also, the radius point has been located.

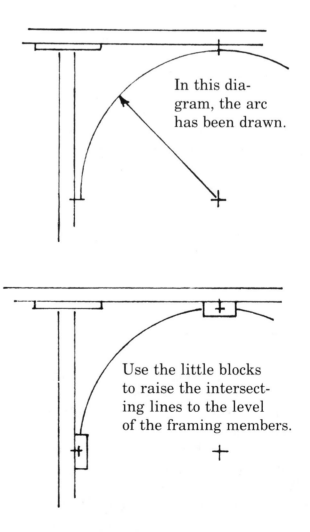

In this diagram, the arc has been drawn.

Use the little blocks to raise the intersecting lines to the level of the framing members.

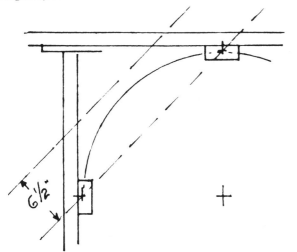

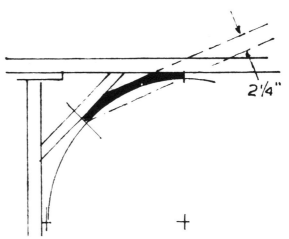

This diagram is a preliminary arch sweep study. With the parallel rule or a couple of yardsticks parallel to one another see what the distance is between a line passing through the spring and crown points and a line which would represent the other side of an arch sweep including structure. In this example such an arch sweep would be wasteful of wood and of insufficient strength at the ends.

By adding an arch brace, the length of the sweep is halved, the sweep is stronger, and much wood is saved. To locate the brace, cut one end of a piece of 1½" + scrap at 45° and slide the batten about until it is exactly ¾" from the arc. Mark and cut and insert with 6 penny nails through lead holes. The arch sweep stock is now reduced to 2¼". The large scale drawing below shows a piece of this stock being marked.

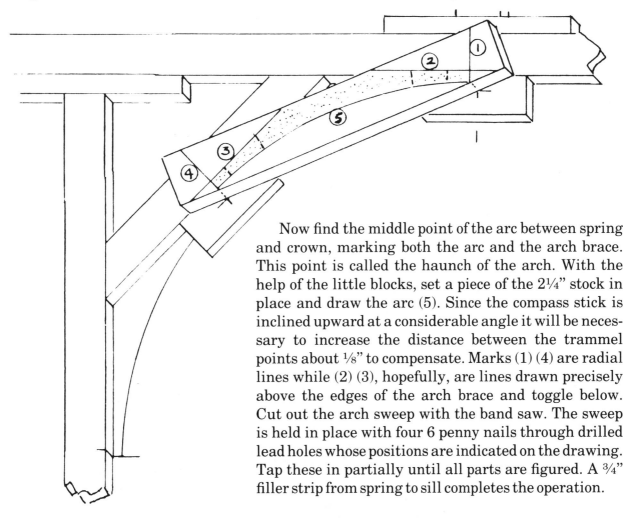

Now find the middle point of the arc between spring and crown, marking both the arc and the arch brace. This point is called the haunch of the arch. With the help of the little blocks, set a piece of the 2¼" stock in place and draw the arc (5). Since the compass stick is inclined upward at a considerable angle it will be necessary to increase the distance between the trammel points about ⅛" to compensate. Marks (1) (4) are radial lines while (2) (3), hopefully, are lines drawn precisely above the edges of the arch brace and toggle below. Cut out the arch sweep with the band saw. The sweep is held in place with four 6 penny nails through drilled lead holes whose positions are indicated on the drawing. Tap these in partially until all parts are figured. A ¾" filler strip from spring to sill completes the operation.

A Whimsical Arrangement
 of Folding Arches

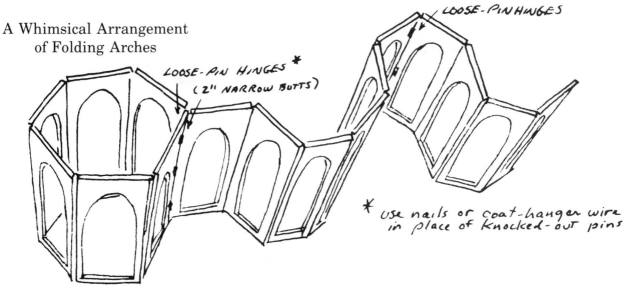

Most archways in folding scenery occur in modular sets with panels of equal width for easy handling. In such cases a maximum opening is desirable, and the panel frame will have only one set of stiles, common both to the archway and the overall frame. While the arch construction is the same, the manner of layout is somewhat different, as diagrammed below.

need not be known numerically, just transferred off and used. It is the practical distance which will secure the maximum archway within the particular panel, and a designer should avoid specifying it numerically in such an instance. For example, should a radius be specified a few inches smaller for some reason, the width of the common stile will have to be increased, usually by shimming up, which is a bother.

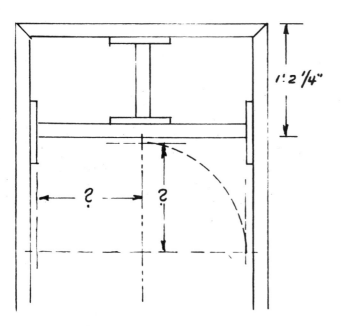

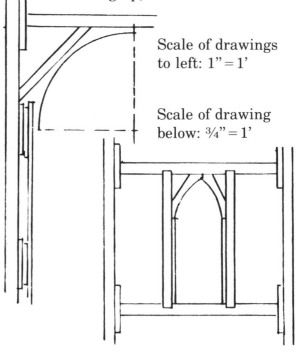

Scale of drawings
to left: 1” = 1’

Scale of drawing
below: ¾” = 1’

The panel shown is 2’-9” wide with the top of the archway specified 1’-3” below the top of the frame. Establish the centerline and draw in the lines ¾” from the toggle and stiles as indicated. Set the trammel points at (?) distance. (?) is a distance that

Of course, if a considerably smaller opening is involved, such as the lancet window shown above right, inner stiles will be used and there is no problem.

While on the subject of windows in flat-framed panels, in order to have clear openings at right-angled corners, notched joints must be substituted for shoes. Notches from ¾" to ⅞" deep bring the inner stiles within the effective reach of the 8 penny nails.

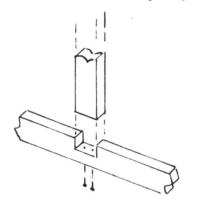

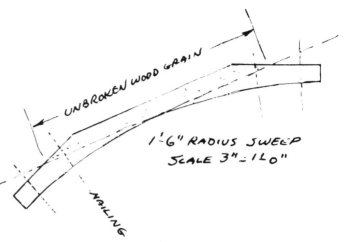

Sill pieces for archway panels are made from 1¼" battens. The joints connecting stiles and sill are half joints as sketched below. Set the table saw blade at ⅜" and rake out these joints. If you are doing a considerable number of such joints, you might do well to purchase a set of dado blades.

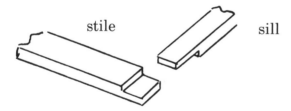

The method for a practical arch sweep has been given, but not the rationale for this particular approach. In my own experience, this solution has been the most resisted of all my construction techniques, yet I know of no alternative technique which satisfies the requirements for strength and economy and is of a soft wood for easy stapling.

On the preceding page the small lancet window has only a radius of 9", so there are but two arch sweeps. However, when the radius goes beyond 12", arch braces should be introduced so that the number of sweeps can be increased, thus reducing the width of the sweep stock as well as strengthening the arch. As the large-scale drawing of the

sweep shows, the important thing is how much wood grain runs clear through unbroken by the arc. And one set of holding nails must pass through this clear run. It goes without saying that these nails must pass through this clear run. And it should go without saying that the lead holes for these nails should always be drilled slightly larger so that there is no danger of splitting.

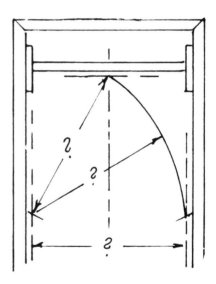

Another popular arch is the gothic, for which the radius is exactly the width of the opening and, in this particular sketch, the (?) which accompanies the "maximum opening in a specified screen pack panel." Proceed as before, then transfer the distance between the vertical lines to the trammel points and from the crown intersection strike arcs across the vertical lines. These intersections will be the radius points. Arch braces are cut at 30° and 60°. Bisect the chord between the spring and crown and draw a line from the opposing radius point through this intersection to find the juncture of the arch sweeps.

Fabric Covering
Liners

Many fabrics, especially burlap, are translucent if not semi-transparent, and a liner of some opaque material must be used where open framework is involved. Two layers of 60- or 70-pound Kraft paper or four layers of newsprint are sufficient. In the case of newsprint, these layers must be laminated with wheat paste to be of sufficient strength.

If the frames are to be covered on both sides, liners must also be placed on both sides. Besides the problem of transparency or translucency, the pattern of the frame beneath the burlap can be detected without liners since the wood is light in color and will show through while the open spaces between the framing members will appear darker. Theoretically, a layer of heavy Kraft paper on each side would suffice in this situation, but two layers together are so much less liable to get torn that I prefer two layers as a liner on each side to be covered and have found the additional expense well worth it.

Kraft papers lighter than 60 pound tend to rattle and tear easily and are not satisfactory in any respect. If such must be used in an emergency, additional layers will be required.

If paper is to be the liner, then it must be remembered that paper, unlike fabric, is rigid. So the four corners must be stapled first, one long side to begin with, and so on.

With flat-framing, the liner is then stapled down everywhere there is a batten

below, at 6" to 8" intervals. Avoid running a finger along the paper as this will cause small bulges to build up. Trimming is done with the utility knife, held with the fingers of the hand only, while the thumb acts as a guide, feeling the edge of the frame below.

On flat frames to be joined for folding, liners are trimmed back about ⅛" to maintain clean edges. When burlap is brought up around an edge with a liner cut flush or protruding, the liner is caught up and small bumps or ridges are caused. Such irregularities will show from the audience.

On slab frames, the liner must overlap by 1" to 1½" any edges, with the exception of curves where sweeps occur. Staple the liner down at the four corners, as before, then snip the corners as shown in the diagrams below. Fold the liner down and staple in from the sides. Battens turned on edge do not provide sufficient area for the liner to be secured properly along the ¾" faces.

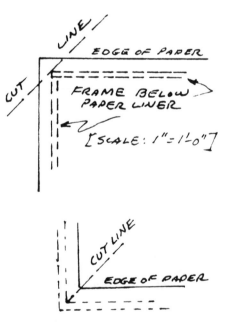

Where there are frames wider than the recommended 36" Kraft paper stock, sheets must be overlapped and often taped. The diagram on the next page shows the size and structural characteristics of the slab, and, alongside to the right, the paper overlaps.

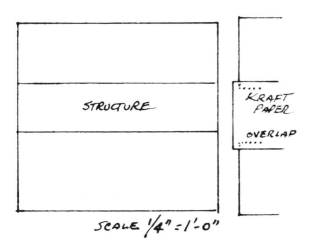

STRUCTURE

KRAFT PAPER

OVERLAP

SCALE ¼" = 1'-0"

Tape that is not the same color as the paper will show through, so such tape must be hidden by being placed on the back side.

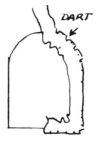

DART

Covering Slabs

Before covering the slab with burlap, the window reveal must be faced separately. Use a 4" burlap strip to form an open sleeve as shown in the diagram. This must be done for two reasons. First, the covering burlap cannot be pulled around and through to the back of such a small curved opening, and, second, there is the problem with the corners of the window, as the application of the liner has already shown. Such a thick facing is necessary not only for nearly all interior openings but for a goodly number of exterior profiles as well, such as castle crenelations and other irregular shapes.

There are two ways of joining the more useful 3' (+ or −) burlap strips when wider pieces are needed: by sewing or by stapling to a common batten. For this particlar slab, sewing is the better solution. If stapling to

common battens had been desired, the slab would have been structured differently in anticipation of it.

For each side cut three pieces about 8'-3" long and sew them together with plain seams. Commence covering by stapling a selvage down about ½" back from the slab edge and then bring the fabric around the end and across the face to the other side. Turn under excess at top and bottom as it will not be necessary to cover the top or bottom of the slab. Since burlap stretches somewhat you may have more than enough to reach to the other edge of the slab, but as long as stapling here is within ½" of the edge it does not matter how the edge is finished since the next piece will lie over it. The diagram shows the positions of the two pieces.

The main thing is that the vertical seams be straight, for then the seams tend to disappear in the mind's eye, at least. Often I use taut strings stretched between nails as guides. Once the sides are secured, tuck under the excess burlap, top and bottom, and staple. Do not staple in one direction across top or bottom, rather divide and subdivide so that any fullness is absorbed in place rather than being shifted along. Staples should be about ½" apart and so close to the edge of the burlap that the fabric cannot be rolled back, for any ridge catches light. Crease edges flat where burlap has been tucked under, using a smooth piece of metal or the bottom plate of the Swingline 101 stapler. The bottom plate of the Arrow JT-21 is unsuitable. Remember that of all the errors found in the fabrication of self-supporting scenery, the worst, from an audience viewpoint, are poorly stapled edges.

Commence the covering for the other side in the same manner, stapling the selvage

½" from the edge of the slab, thus covering the raw burlap edge below, then bring the material around the slab and across the other face, carrying it to within ⅛" of the slab edge, and finishing it neatly. If the burlap is to be turned under, there being enough of it to do so, cut off the selvage edge first.

After the slab is completely covered, place temporary staples around the window and remove the window portion, leaving about ½" over. By snipping in ½" at the corners and around the arch, the burlap can be tucked under itself and the perimeters of the arch window neatly finished on both sides. Then remove the temporary holding staples. The one-inch clamping slot is opened up in the same manner.

The burlap for this particular slab should be all of one color, for the slab is a dimensional monolithic entity in its own right as the terminator of the twofold and is obviously a vital part of the self-support system. A separate color on one side would appear as poorly motivated veneer. On the other hand, a separate color suggesting the interior on one face of the twofold would be quite accceptable because these pieces do not assume the same abstract quality as the slab. And to extend the interior color of the twofold onto that part of the slab which is, in effect, a continuation of the interior, is to act in obedience to the discipline of a realism that is nonexistent in space staging, not to mention the phony appearance.

Joining and Covering Flat-Folds

On page 17, the need for a small backing screen for the archway of the two-fold unit was established, and a fourfold with 2' x 6'-9" panels was specified. These frames should be lined and covered first since this is a "regular" unit and quite typical of the many modular folding screens necessary to any space staging operation, even prior to the consideration of custom-designed items for a particular play.

Unless there is a good reason to the contrary, the covering of sets of folds on both sides is always advisable. One exception is shown in the example sketched below; the folding screen is of yellow burlap on which desert plants of green burlap have been stitched with heavy yarn. To do this, access to the rear of the covering and liner is necessary.

On pages 2 and 3 the reversible flap hinge was described in terms of paper assembly. The hinge in cloth is similar, but far less tedious. On the masking fourfold I would recommend using the same color as the slab for the edging strips, cloth flap hinges and the covering on one side. And for the other side, the color should match that selected for the interior side of the twofold. The interior color would be seen through the archway when the *Set for Simple Dwelling* was turned for an exterior scene.

Cut four pieces of burlap of the slab color about 7' + long. Each joint requires two 3" edging strips and one 4" hinge strip. These strips can be taken from the pieces already cut and still leave enough for the covering. Now, with the 3" strips, edge all the stiles that are to be joined together.

Lay a 4" hinge strip alongside one of the frames and cut this strip one inch shorter than the height of the frame. Fold the strip over, halving it, then halve the remaining, then halve it again, and crease all folds. Open the strip up, lay flat, and make the hinge pieces by cutting where creased, following the weave. This will make eight pieces, each approximately 10" long. Put these aside in one pile and repeat for the other two hinging strips. *Do not mix the pieces from pile to pile.* In this way, you will not have to calculate the exact measurements of these pieces, nor do the pieces have to be exactly the same length.

Place the two frames side by side. Lay the first hinge flap in position and staple down as shown in the diagram.

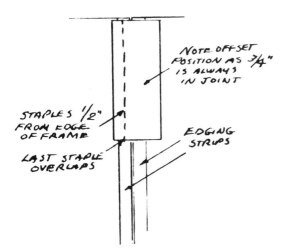

NOTE OFFSET POSITION AS 3/4" IS ALWAYS IN JOINT

STAPLES 1/2" FROM EDGE OF FRAME

LAST STAPLE OVERLAPS

EDGING STRIPS

Since this stapling not only holds the burlap to the frame but will also hold the frames together, this is a good time to explain how the staple gun is held to ensure maximum security. Cant the gun slightly forward and *compress* the handle. All too often, a person with a weak grip will push the handle down rather than compressing it, so that the gun cants backward and the staple is not driven all the way in. If you can insert your fingernail under the staple,

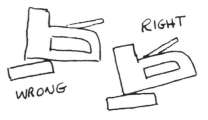

WRONG   RIGHT

it has not been properly driven. The bridge of the staple is what binds the material, not the legs!

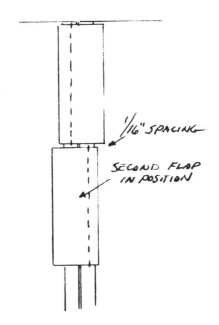

1/16" SPACING

SECOND FLAP IN POSITION

Note that the second flap is placed about 1/16" away from the first. This is to prevent the flaps from tearing at one another as the frames are folded, since one hinge is rolling in a direction opposite to the other. This spacing was compensated for when the strip was cut about 1" shorter than the height of the frames.

Nor can a hinge be flush with the top or bottom since a staple must overlap the end of each flap to prevent raveling. The raw ends of hinge flaps *cannot* be turned under since they show to both sides. The only other solution to raveling is to prepare strips of cloth from 8" to 10" wide, overcast these edges on a sewing machine that has a zigzag control, then cut these strips into 4" pieces.

When all the hinge flaps are in place, turn the frames over and place them side by side again, but slightly apart. Pull up the loose ends of the flaps through this wide crack, then push the frames together and staple the flaps down. Be sure you staple a flap to the stile to which it is not already attached. Before stapling, test each flap to be sure there is no hidden fullness underneath the frames — burlap is notorious for not pulling around and up easily. It is also very important that the frames be perfectly aligned — there is not as much play in the fabric hinge as one might think. Be sure the hinge flaps are taut, but not so taut that you have pulled the frames out of parallel, for this will prevent the frames from folding all the way in both directions.

When the two panels are joined, then it is best to cover the "lead" panel. With a pencil, mark a line about ½" back from the lead edge, staple a selvage edge along this line and then bring the burlap around the lead edge and across the panel, *never* the other way — that is, commencing at the hinge joint and then bringing the material across the panel and around to the rear of the lead edge — for this will require temporary stapling on the lead stile in order to get the tension correct. Fold the other panel under and out of the way. Never attempt to finish an edge with another panel lying alongside as the latter will interfere with the proper position of the staple gun, which, when at the edge of a frame, should be so canted that the staple is driven slightly inward.

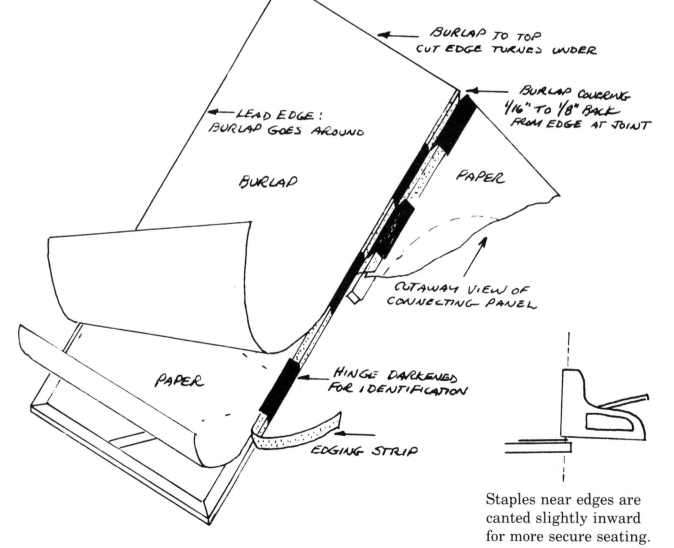

BURLAP TO TOP
CUT EDGE TURNED UNDER

BURLAP COVERING
¼₆" TO ⅛" BACK
FROM EDGE AT JOINT

LEAD EDGE:
BURLAP GOES AROUND

BURLAP

PAPER

CUTAWAY VIEW OF
CONNECTING PANEL

PAPER

HINGE DARKENED
FOR IDENTIFICATION

EDGING STRIP

Staples near edges are canted slightly inward for more secure seating.

Complete the covering of the panel along the hinge side by starting at the center and working out along the stile in both directions, turning the excess under and pulling the burlap taut. If the excess is more than an inch or so, cut a strip off so you will not have a lot of burlap lying underneath. Keep the edge of the burlap from 1/16" to 1/8" back from the edge of the frame where joints are involved, otherwise the hinge action is impaired and the burlap edge is caught up in the rolling action and turned up. Also keep the staples as close to the edge of the burlap as possible. Do not pull the material so taut that you get a scalloped edge, nor leave it so slack that it will sag when the unit is erected. When you come to the ends be sure that the material is neatly tucked under. When working with the ends a light fullness will develop. Commence at center, then subdivide over and over again, and the fullness will disappear. Never staple across an end in one direction or this fullness will be carried along and build up to an amount that cannot be seated evenly.

Now cover the reverse side of the lead panel with the interior color. Here it does not matter which long side is commenced first, though I would recommend placing the selvage over the burlap already along the lead edge. Then take the other two frames and do likewise. Finally, the two pairs of frames are joined to form the fourfold, and the four remaining panel sides can be covered. A pair of workers helps because there is so much refolding. And it may be necessary to cover the work table with Kraft paper to keep the burlap clean.

Covering the Two-Fold and Clamping Strip

Prepare edging strips and hinge flaps of the prime, or slab, color and join the clamp-

ing strip, end panel and archway panel. With the prime color, cover lead edge and "outside" face of the end panel. On the archway panel, stapled rather than sewn burlap joints will be employed. But first run an edging strip of the prime color around the inner stiles and arch sweeps of the archway. This will simplify the fitting of the five pieces of fabric, as shown in the diagram. Study the detailed diagram of the stapled joint.

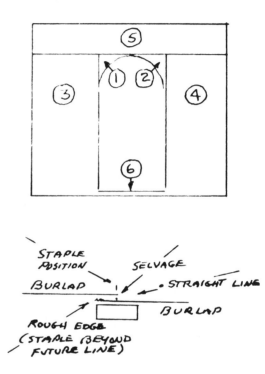

While it is possible to crease a turned-under edge and fit it to the straight line you have drawn along the burlap underneath, using a selvage edge is recommended for beginners. Again, neatness decreases the visibility of the joint, in the same way that keeping a sewn joint straight renders it nearly invisible. The sill (6) is covered by a strip of burlap secured with white glue, and trimmed when dry. I recommend the prime color here on all three faces, for it would look strange to carry the interior color across the threshold.

This completes the Stagecraft I section. The shutters for this set piece are covered in Stagecraft II.

SCENE DESIGN

From the Picture into Space

A scene design is a scheme for making scenery which tells an audience something important about a play's environment. It may be a sketch, a model, a diagram, or even an idea. The design itself need not have any inherent artistic value. It is given significance only when the scenery created from it proves successful in productions.

The scene design spectrum ranges from a transcription of literal environment to highly interpretive scenic elements. Scenery for proscenium staging may run the complete gamut between these extremes, but scenery used in open staging cannot. This scenery is *always* interpretive in basic conception, no matter how literal details of it may be.

For literal environments, "slices of life" are simply moved over to the "framed" stage. The pair of sketches shows how the "slice" P-P becomes the picture or proscenium plane. Interpretation may be added by "styling" these slices of life, though such interpretation is entirely optional.

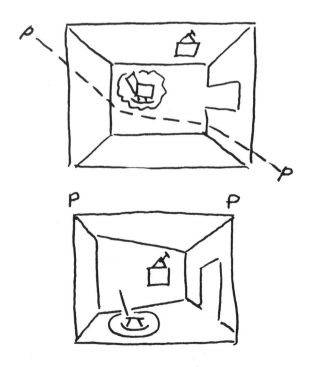

But when the environment is moved out into real space, there is no P-P cut line and matching proscenium frame to organize it. Decisions as to overall shape and size have to be made that do not have to be made in

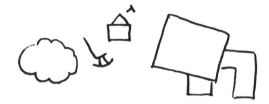

the proscenium example shown. This is what we mean when we say that, *fundamentally,* the scene design is always interpretive regardless of whether the wallpaper detailing

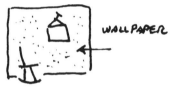

is the same for both examples. By interpretation is meant the selection of important details and the reorganization of them into art forms *in their own right,* and not as so many pieces of a jigsaw puzzle making up a complete picture but having little meaning by themselves.

Before going on to a discussion of the sort of design concepts which apply to working in space, and some typical production solutions, a little philosophy about scene design in general will be helpful.

Some Philosophy

One should bear in mind that each piece of scenery on the stage is an artifact of man and not "the real thing." Even if a tree has been cut down and moved to the stage, it is still arranged and illuminated by the artist, and so bears his mark . . . his desire, so to speak, to make a statement about a tree. In short, scenery is a visual language, conveying meaning.

What is a *language*? It is a method of communication between people who share things in common, such as a cultural tradition or a community of interests. It is like a bridge between people over which ideas, moods and emotions flow back and forth. Some examples are the *language* of art, the *language* of love, the English *language*, the *language* of mathematics, etc.

To continue the analogy of the bridge, when a language is functioning properly, the structural configuration of the bridge is taken for granted. In fact, those in communication with one another may be completely unaware of the bridge, as a young child starting to talk or a person tapping out a rhythm in response to a lively piece of music. The child doesn't know grammar as such, though he uses it. The person listening to the music may never have seen a sheet of musical notation or played an instrument. Even when the language is one that has been learned, such as reading, as opposed to conversation, the imagery jumps full-blown off the page, unaccompanied by the alphabet. An audience is in the position of a person who can read a book without necessarily knowing how to write one.

There are very few people who can describe with any degree of accuracy a setting they have seen on the stage, and with good reason, for the "intentionality" of the artistic experience precedes in importance the actual detailing of it. "Intentionality" is a metaphysical term descriptive of the mind's prime function, the natural application of *meaning* to things. Because a person fails to describe accurately the setting he has seen the night before need not imply that the meaning of it has escaped him. Anyone who has even so much as glanced at children's post-production sketches of scenery cannot fail to see "intentionality" at work quite naturally and without self-consciousness.

Note also how children make open stage scenery fit the shape of a piece of paper, unconsciously taking dimensional set pieces out of a volume of space and translating them into proper picture imagery. The reverse process applies to sketches for open stage scenery. Such sketches should be reworked into small set piece models before the design goes to the shop for construction. A wise designer begins his study directly with cardboard, scissors and glue rather than with pencil and sketch pad.

The foregoing brings up the subject of dimensionality on the stage. For the purposes of discussion, let us place the strictly pictorial at one end of the design spectrum and the strictly sculptural at the other, or "picture" vs. "statue." The picture consists of a flat plane, while the statue is multiplaned, so to speak. The picture can be framed. If the statue is framed, the real space around it must be included, so it becomes a diorama rather than a picture *per se*. If not framed, then the statue exists within whatever contains that particular volume of space, such as an art gallery.

Notice the wide variety of frames for pictures. The more realistic the picture the more ornate the frame will be, while abstract paintings will have simpler frames, or, with non-objective paintings, possibly none at all. The frame protects the "atmospheric" quality of a painting. When realistic illusion does not exist, such protection is unnecessary and a frame redundant. In a diorama, the foreground objects are already in space, so the frame protects only the panorama. If the panorama is removed, then the frame can be dispensed with, and the display now takes the form of a sand table.

The arena stage can be likened to a sand table. The audience sits around the stage, and there is no vertical background to deal with. Move the seats away from one or more sides of the stage, and there is background, as in an art gallery where displays are set near a wall. On many open stages, this background is merely the continuation of the theatre chamber. Where such a background is specifically decorated for a particular play, some sort of framing is required to separate it from the architecture of the theatre chamber. This situation can be likened to the diorama. A working stagehouse with proscenium frame is merely an intensification of the diorama example. In an earlier section we saw the example of a framed box setting. When the frame was removed, the setting had to be converted to a set piece. If this set piece were to remain on a proscenium stage, then some sort of background, such as a cyclorama, would be necessary, and this, in turn, would be framed by the proscenium.

Design Factors for Open Staging

(1) **Profile.** It is apparent from the foregoing that every setting in an open space will have an overall profile. Good designers use this fact to advantage. Some silhouettes are so descriptive that further detailing is optional.

Spanish House

New England
Saltbox House

(2) **The Abstract.** The process by which a picture from the wall is converted into a statue in space is one which results in the subject matter being treated in a more *abstract* manner. This is of significance to the open-stage designer for several reasons:

(a) Locales of scenes are freely established, often just through the use of props . . .

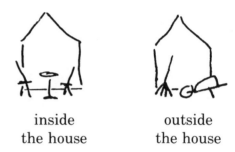

| inside | outside |
| the house | the house |

(b) There is a considerable degree of freedom in the organization of detail when abstraction is pronounced. Here are some stage trees, for example . . .

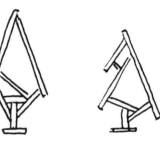

Trees of 1x2s backed with
fabric used in Nordic and
Oriental fairy tales.

Tree for *Noye's Fludde* —
rug tube and 30 degrees
tilt disc with
fabric streamers

Useful threefold screen
depicting forest and hut.

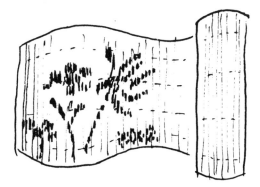

A forest of
ceremonial
fan shapes,
covered with
green fabric
and excised
with bamboo
details, with
dew suggested
by crystals.

Woods scene for *Emperor's Nightingale.*

A woodland serpentine shape made
from a rolling blind with foliage
of dyed felt strips glued on.

One of the more difficult design mandates involves actors climbing up into or appearing in trees. The traditional "jungle gym" solution of 2 x 4s with glue-soaked burlap sheathing, though practical, is most cumbersome in handling, transport and storage. Combining the tree with some sort of masking element such as the garden wall sketched below provides space for the use of a step ladder or other elevator, thus returning the tree elements to simple profiles.

(c) An abstract style permits symbols to represent objects that are very large in real life, such as the castle taken from the 15th-century religious play, *The Castle of Per-*

serverance, or the castle from a Joseph Young mosaic (sketch on next page).

Otherwise, the only way to handle large objects on the stage is by way of the proscenium technique of suggestion by showing only a part of the whole object.

FROM A JOSEPH YOUNG MOSAIC

(d) Abstract modules are easily *accessorized*, thus stretching the budget . . .

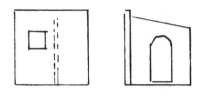

The sketches show the use of just one face of a T-slab unit.

   adobe house

   adobe church

   Spanish house

African hut

   garden wall

French mansion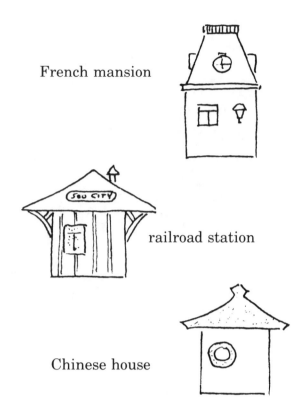

railroad station

Chinese house

. . . and finally . . .

 (e) Since the camera is a framing device, obviously a *picture* of any space-centered scenery is a contradiction in style. Don't show a snapshot of your space setting to the Man from Missouri and expect him to believe it!

Scenery for space staging is designed to be seen by the human eye, and the pictorial impression is assembled in a very different manner than that of the camera. Imagine a porch on a sunny afternoon, with a woven blind extended. The mind sees a complete garden scene, while the camera would record the fact that the slats of the blind obscure the greater part of it.

(3) **Size.** In space, the designer inherits the profile, *and therefore controls the magnitude* of a setting. This means . . .

(a) Big scenery for big actors, and small scenery for small actors . . .

Shown at right are two sets drawn at the same scale of ⅛" = 1'. The hut is from a youth production of *Hansel and Gretel*, while the arch facade is an old warhorse of accessorization and includes such operas as *Don Giovanni*, *Faust* and *Rigoletto*.

(b) A large permanent piece of scenery for scenes with many actors, and a piece or two for smaller scenes . . .

See also the section on Scenic Progression for a more detailed explanation of the workings of these sets.

VIGAS TO SUPPORT INSIDE DECOR FRAMES

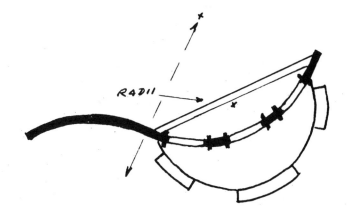

RADII

VILLAGE WELL

Scale: ⅛" = 1'

(c) Scenery here and there for the wandering in and out of scenes during the course of a play . . .

The diagram below represents a hypothetical play about a weekend at the seashore. There are three scenes: the beach, a street cafe, and a church, in that order

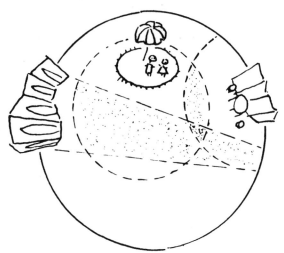

A setting for Lope de Vega's *Fuenteovejuna*. Some dozen scenes, located both in the village of Fuenteovejuna and about the surrounding countryside, include rooms in various houses, palaces and castles, in fields, by waysides, and in the village square. The elliptical archways were accessorized with grills, doors and curtains.

and all in the same town. Beach activity, then dusk and romance, followed by supper *al fresco*. A wedding the next morning. All scenes involve passersby in varying numbers. Shaded areas represent the "shared space" made possible by the fact that the settings are *focal points* to which the actors relate rather than having a series of complete sets, proscenium-style.

(d) There is a tendency to over-design scenery. A good rule of thumb is to make scenery as compact as possible. A few inches here, a foot or two there all add up. Compare the area of a 4' x 8' panel (32 square feet) with that of one of our typical folding screen panels, 2'-9" x 7'-3" (20 square feet). One third more cost, for what? A panel set up in space will appear larger than a panel of the same size that is part of a continuity such as flats in a box set. Thus, a 6' x 12' unit is sufficiently large for opera, while most modular folding screens will not average over 8' in height.

Just how small can scenery be and still in proper scale with actors? In the cottage scene the rear wall is only 5½' high. Yet this setting has seen action with adult actors in such productions as *The Unwicked Witch, Maggie's Magic Teapot, The Old Maid and the Thief,* and *Let's Make an Opera.*

(e) A further aspect of size control is that much modern art which would be overwhelming in the full pictorial extension of a proscenium frame stage is entirely acceptable as freestanding scenery when its scale is properly balanced to the human scale.

(4) **Space Staging Within the Proscenium Arch.** This is a practice already established in proscenium stagecraft. Units of such scenery are called "set pieces." The same rules apply: (a) profiled units, (b) *always* a "cushion of space" around the set pieces, and (c) a total enclosure such as curtains or a sky cyclorama. While the set pieces do not require the proscenium frame for their resolution, the curtains or cyclorama will. One is reminded of a store window display which follows the principles of open rather than proscenium staging despite the fact the window makes a very strong "frame." Such display is usually dimensional, in a "cushion of space," backed in turn by clean, "architectural" backgrounds of panels or plain, seamless colored paper. See the Architectural Section for a further discussion of proscenium staging along the lines of store window display.

(5) The principles of **Cubism** and **Collage** apply to space staging. Cubism is the art of the multiple close-up. Collage is a way to

show things without having to resort to fac-simile. Both eliminate "perspective" and, consequently, "atmosphere" as we are accustomed to knowing them in painting and in illusionary scenery. This does not mean that "atmosphere" in the wider sense of the term cannot be created on a platform stage, but that it is literally "built up" in a different manner and, as such, is suggestive rather than illusionary.

(6) **Evaluate the Playing Space** for what it is, so that the scenery may properly relate to it. For example, if the playing space is a beautiful ballroom, then the scenery must be skillfully crafted and neatly finished, with an emphasis on heavily textured fabrics, preferably dyed and, if decorated, lightly dry-brushed or chalked. If the playing space is a nondescript studio, painted muslin might be OK. The idea is, anything in space cannot help but be related to that which makes the space.

(7) "With a little bit o' luck . . ." **Someone Else Will Build the Bloomin' Set.** Bucking down a design to the shop may work well in the proscenium theatre with its "flats," rigged backdrops and applied decor, but it is not the best way to go about preparing scenery for space staging. There is a necessity for craft information input in the design process itself. When scenery must stand by itself in space, it seems as though structure and detail are transparently overlapped. Thus, a thorough knowledge of set construction is often the springboard to design rather than the servant of it.

(8) Determining just **How Much Scenery** is needed is one of the big challenges in open staging. This is tied in with two other factors — the nature of the performance area and the nature of human vision. The ultimate in performance areas, I believe, is a finished space into which just what is needed can be placed without the unused area appearing "empty." As to human vision, we must remember that though man's  eyes cannot see behind him, he does not think of the world to the rear as black or empty, but as continuing around him.

Once the basic proposition is understood of introducing only that scenery which is needed into an open space otherwise dressed and already complete, one moves easily towards simplicity. On the proscenium stage simplicity is not so readily achieved, for the "picture frame" induces a complete transcription, whether it is desired or not, and the separation of extraneous from essential detail can prove most difficult. In this respect, in addition to a clean stage with curtains or a sky cyclorama, not inexpensive items in themselves if done properly, interpretive platforming goes a long way towards nullifying the proscenium influence.

Further Production Examples

It has been my experience that a major challenge for many people with space stages is the redesigning of settings which have already been designed and staged within the proscenium frame, and, of these, the most difficult are the room interiors or so-called "box" settings.

The problem here is psychological: the influence of prior example. Without knowing how someone else had gone about staging a play, particularly under different circumstances, one could only create a practical design for the circumstances at hand. I have often heard directors say that they always remove from purchased scripts all photographs and production diagrams *prior* to distribution to members of the staff, cast and crews.

Most interior settings can be solved in terms of standard sets of folding screens, both arches and opaques, or combinations thereof. (The design factors for many useful shapes are discussed in the Stagecraft II section.)

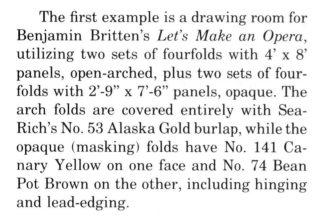

The first example is a drawing room for Benjamin Britten's *Let's Make an Opera*, utilizing two sets of fourfolds with 4' x 8' panels, open-arched, plus two sets of four-folds with 2'-9" x 7'-6" panels, opaque. The arch folds are covered entirely with Sea-Rich's No. 53 Alaska Gold burlap, while the opaque (masking) folds have No. 141 Canary Yellow on one face and No. 74 Bean Pot Brown on the other, including hinging and lead-edging.

Tapestry and bookcase panels closing three of the arches were executed by dry brushing on Alaska Gold burlap, then stapled to the rear of the arch frames. Heavy Kraft paper overlaid to the rear prevented see-through. The firebox and mantle of the fireplace were made as a three-dimensional insert, while the effect of a mirror was created by dry-brushing on Eggshell White burlap stapled to the rear of the arch frame. The windows were of open muntin framework inserted flush in the archways and backed by heavy gauze to receive light for sunlight and moonlight effects. The archway to the rear of the piano was closed by two of the yellow panels of one set of masking screens, with the remaining panels turned brown side out to terminate the set. The other set of masking screens formed the hallway backing at the other end of the set. The open archway here was dressed with portieres. By removing the fireplace insert, the set was reduced to four folding units for instant removal for a scene change.

For the other scene of this Britten opera, a children's playroom upstairs, the setting shown on page 38 was used. Since the playroom scene is shown in process of erection for a "rehearsal" scene as well as completed for a "performance" scene later on, the folding and clamping techniques are a delight for the audience to watch.

This particular production of *Let's Make an Opera* illustrates *both* modular and repetitive folding screens that are highly accessorized and a custom-designed setting so typical of certain types of interiors that it can be used over and over again with a minimum of accessory changes.

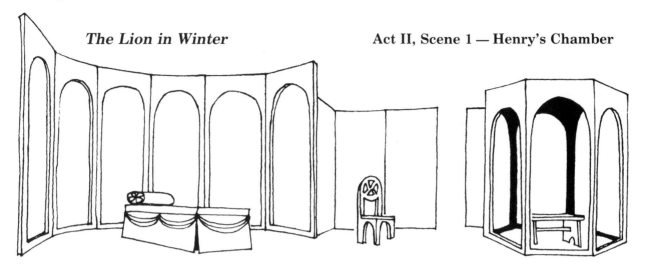

The Lion in Winter   Act II, Scene 1 — Henry's Chamber

Sketches by Dan Hanley

Obviously there are many uses for plain and arch screen sets in their pure or relatively unadulterated forms, and, for an example of this, I am indebted to Paul Ebert and his screens for *Lion in Winter*, and their use forever and a day thereafter!

Paul Ebert, director of the Oak Ridge Community Playhouse in Tennessee, built his production of *Lion in Winter* around five sets of folding screens, devised as shown below. Each unit was completely double-covered with burlap in the color indicated. Paul said that the next time around he would prefer 9' instead of 10' for the height of the taller panels. A diagram of Ebert's stage, and a complete plot of each scene, are given on the following pages. A crew of six men and two women, black-clad, handled the screens and props, working under dim backlighting in full view of the audience. The shifts took anywhere from one-half to one minute apiece.

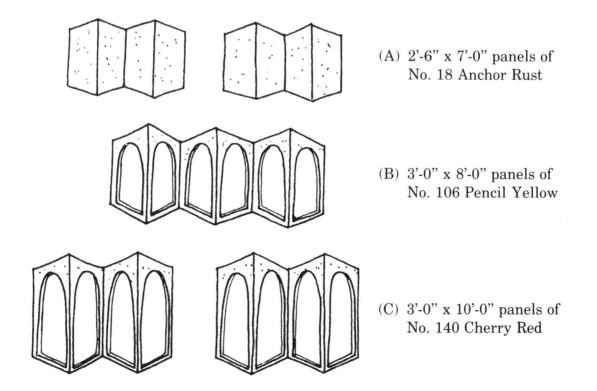

(A) 2'-6" x 7'-0" panels of
    No. 18 Anchor Rust

(B) 3'-0" x 8'-0" panels of
    No. 106 Pencil Yellow

(C) 3'-0" x 10'-0" panels of
    No. 140 Cherry Red

Seven sets of fourfold masking
screens placed as a nonshifting
background beyond the area of
selective illumination.

Panels 3' x 14'
Tropic Sky burlap

Ebert's Economy Open Stage

A nondescript Army post theatre
rehabilitated as a space stage.

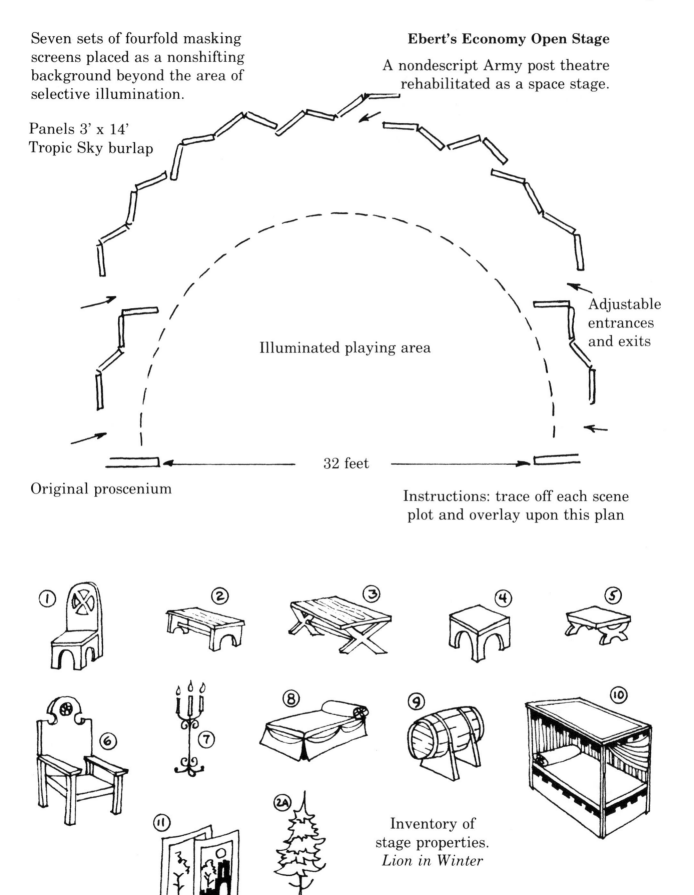

Illuminated playing area

Adjustable
entrances
and exits

32 feet

Original proscenium

Instructions: trace off each scene
plot and overlay upon this plan

Inventory of
stage properties.
Lion in Winter

Complete Technical Plot of Scenes

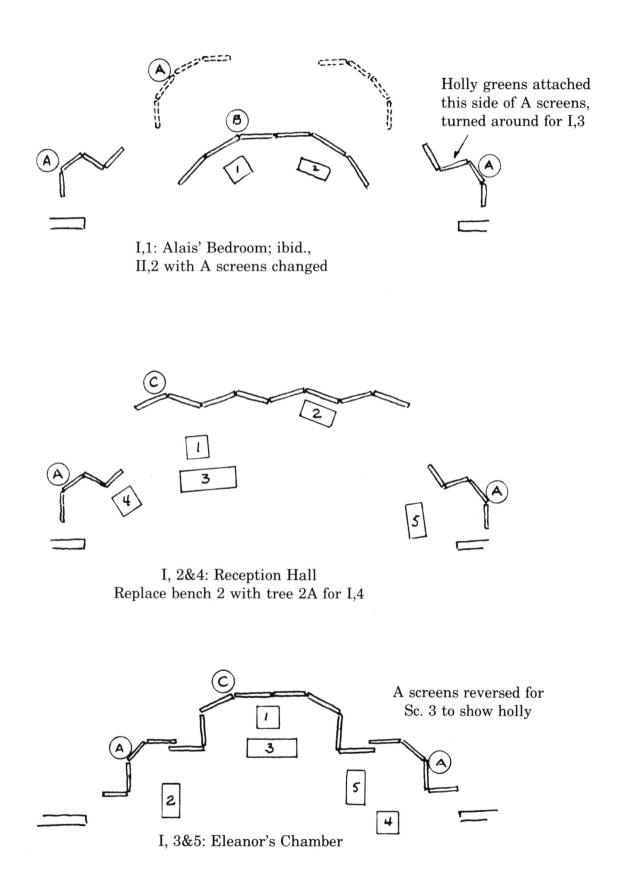

Holly greens attached
this side of A screens,
turned around for I,3

I,1: Alais' Bedroom; ibid.,
II,2 with A screens changed

I, 2&4: Reception Hall
Replace bench 2 with tree 2A for I,4

A screens reversed for
Sc. 3 to show holly

I, 3&5: Eleanor's Chamber

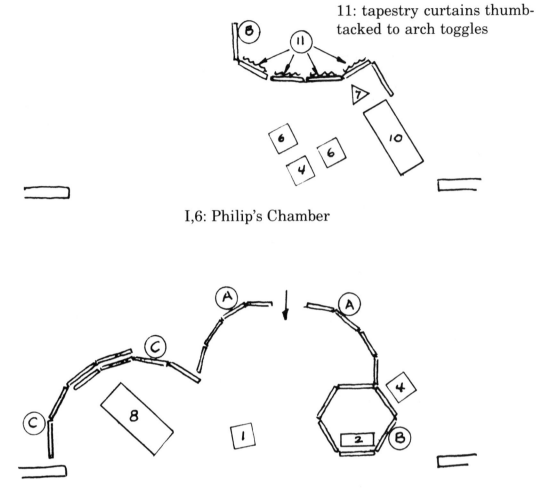

11: tapestry curtains thumb-
tacked to arch toggles

I,6: Philip's Chamber

II,1: Henry's Chamber

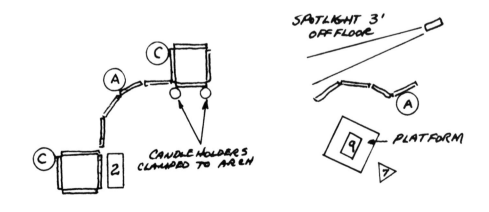

II,3: The Wine Cellar

Commentary

Though this book deals specifically with self-supporting scenery, brief comments are timely regarding Paul Ebert's dramatic lighting techniques for plays such as *Lion in Winter*. Since Ebert prefers an open-stage look, he downplays his proscenium by using ellipsoidal spotlights in the anteproscenium beams overhead, though otherwise fresnel spotlights with high hats (snoots) would be advisable for these positions. For effect, he relies on an abundance of down-, side- and backlighting both by ellipsoidal and fresnel spotlights. It goes without saying that free-standing scenery increases the opportunities for such selective lighting since the scenic units are space-centered and thus do not block off many good lighting positions which would but for this be lost. According to Ebert, Henry's Chamber, II,1, was the single prettiest set, with frontal lighting kept low on the red arches, with cross- and backlighting dim, and with a single fresnel spotlight aimed straight down into the pavilion formed by the B arches.

The Wine Cellar, II,3, was also dimly lit, with heavy shadows everywhere. The special spotlight shown on the plan projected shadows of persons entering on the wall formed by the A screens stage right. Note also the use of candlelight in this scene.

All too often one hears of potential free-standing scenery enthusiasts who end up by compromising the system for lack of time or initiative, declaring they get by without all the effort necessary to make the screens as specified. Their screens are frequently not screens at all, but flats, incapable of the flexibility of properly executed reversible-folding, double-covered planes, and the future uses are limited indeed.

The following excerpts, taken from the correspondence of Paul Ebert, may give heart to others who are hesitant or faltering along the way.

March 14, 1969:

"We had a chamber concert in the Playhouse between week-ends of the performances, so I set up the red arches and rust screens in a double shallow curve effect behind the grand piano and the harpsichord, and it was really pretty. Had many comments on the background, which again was very appropriate to the kind of music being played."

"A local school teacher has nailed me to rent her the yellow six-fold unit for something she's doing with her junior-high kids as it is 'perfect for our little play,' but I haven't decided whether to do it or not; the unit is too valuable . . ."

May 2, 1969:

"Re the *Lion in Winter* screens, a few weeks after that show closed the local ballet people staged their annual recital and performance and ended up using all of them for ballet scenery for one of those typical toyshop numbers, and it came off great; they set up the yellow six-fold with a "bay window" in it, hung swag draperies in the arches and filled in the bottoms of the arch openings with yellow burlap plugs, and it looked quite handsome; also they rigged the big arches with the openings filled in with single pieces of burlap of a contrasting color, using them as a sort of coarse scrim, to very good effect. Such versatility. So far those five screen sets have provided decor for *Lion*, for a chamber music concert and for the ballet, and they'd have gone into the local school production of *Camelot* if I'd let them out, but I drew the line."

February 4, 1971:

"Those *Lion* units are still furbishing things from one end of the town to the other. Some of them went into Christmas programs at local churches . . . the Civic Ballet has used them again this year . . . some of them are going into a stage show by an outside group to whom we're renting the building week after next . . . and so on."

Ebert is enthusiastic about his seven sets of 4' x 14' folding screens for purely masking purposes upstage. These were built many years ago as an overall background for an opera he produced on a local high school stage. After their return to his own playhouse, Ebert has used them almost exclusively in place of the usual curtain sets and cycloramas which back up space stage settings in most proscenium theatres.

Ebert continues in his letter of February 4:

"One thing is for certain: without those seven sets of 14 ft. blue burlap screens we could not operate in this theatre at all. We closed a play last weekend; the children's theatre moved in immediately and performs this weekend. As soon as they are through the local Jewish Community Center moves in with their annual production. The night after their first performance we have a touring string quartet concert, then two more nights of play performance. As soon as the play closes, the Sweet Adelines, a singing group, move in with their annual musical show, and as soon as they are out I move my next regular Playhouse show on stage. And in the midst of all this (February is hell month around here) we have a daytime science seminar for three days. Without the screens and the blacked-out overhead, we could not set and reset the stage for all this activity.

On February 11, Ebert returned some manuscript corrections, adding:

"After my own rehearsal last night I peeked in at the final dress for the Jewish Center play and found they are using the two Anchor Rust 4-folds as the 'set' for a small insert scene . . . This is going to be a blow to the lady who called the other day to rent one of them to use at a church function this weekend. I think I will quit producing plays and just build freestanding scenery and rent out the building to everyone else. It is getting so I can hardly find time in there to put on my own plays."

And on August 29, 1971, Ebert wrote further:

In August a bunch of high school kids here did a production of *Romeo and Juliet* — we gave them the theatre and the equipment and turned them loose. Guess what they used for scenery? Two fourfold red arch units, one sixfold yellow unit and two fourfold reversible screens . . . sound familiar?

It would appear that Paul Ebert is singled out for undue attention. Not so, when it is known that Paul, without benefit of direct instruction, followed specifications for self-supporting scenery to the letter, and that few seldom do! There is yet another reason. His adventures with abstract folding screen sets are typical of those who are willing to go all the way, despite the inconvenience of discipline and the tedium of precision stagecraft.

There are plays where actors must go, or at least give the impression of going, down into cellars or upstairs, as in *Arsenic and Old Lace*, for example, and when these sets are done in space rather than in "box set" style, they are best designed around some strong visual element such as a chimney piece, or roof, along with combinations of skeletal and opaque profiles. One is reminded of both the "cutaway" and "inside-outside" set piece stagings of the 1930s on proscenium-with-cyclorama space stages. In those days, realism was being "restyled," so to speak, but now such design motivation is more along the lines of a purposeful "assemblage" after Picasso.

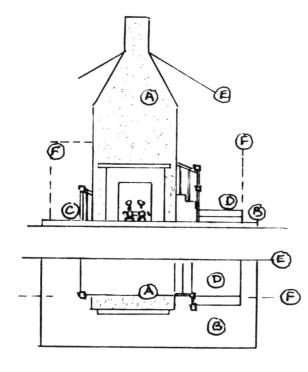

The illustration shows, in abbreviated form, a plan and elevation of just such a central chimney piece (A). By putting the immediate area about the fireplace on an elevated plaza (B) a person descending to the basement by a stair supposedly behind the chimney (C) at least may take one step downward, while the illusion of a stair is further strengthened by a newel post and descending handrail. The illusion of going upstairs is more completely suggested by a couple of risers, a landing (D), and then a step or two in profile. Whether the main house profile lies in plane (E) or in the alcove line (F) is immaterial. If the latter, backings will be necessary for the (E) plane; if the former, the forward alcove planes can be partial panels terminated by likely mouldings.

Some other plays involving parts of houses whose designs can be solved in much the same way are *Dark at the Top of the Stair, Long Day's Journey into Night,* and *Everybody Loves Opal.*

One of the big advantages of any sort of space-centered scenery is the opportunity to continue the visual description of an environment without increasing the size of a particular set piece, such as fog and shoreline prop effects extending a house profile for *Long Day's Journey,* or projected patterns of garden foliage beyond the garden wall setting on the front cover of this book. Or, as has already been demonstrated, room for other action and perhaps other scenic pieces on stage simultaneously.

How Difficult Can It Be?

A person faced with an open stage space once remarked to me, "But I just can't seem to get the scene design started." I asked, "What is the most important feature about this particular set?" The reply was surprisingly simple: "Well, there is this picture on the wall . . ."

I am sure that the kind of wall the person had in mind was not the sort we have been talking about. Rather, it was probably being conceived of as one wall in a "box set," and the problem was not just a matter of hanging a picture on it, but what to do with the side walls with no proscenium frame to end them.

If a wall is all that is required, let it be *just that.* But then, what sort of wall surface? What of the profile? Props? And away we go in a wholly different design direction!

Slabs in basic "T" formation, and, below, the very stable "V-T" plan.

Paint effect of peeling plaster

SIMPLE INTERIOR
note offsetting of props

Cornice, wall paper, chair rail and panelling

A PLUSH ROOM

Spanish peppers

Hand-smoothed appliqué of jiffy papier-mâché sprayed with base color, accent colors dry-brushed

PLAN

interior-exterior idiom

shingles, board & batten

FARMHOUSE INTERIOR

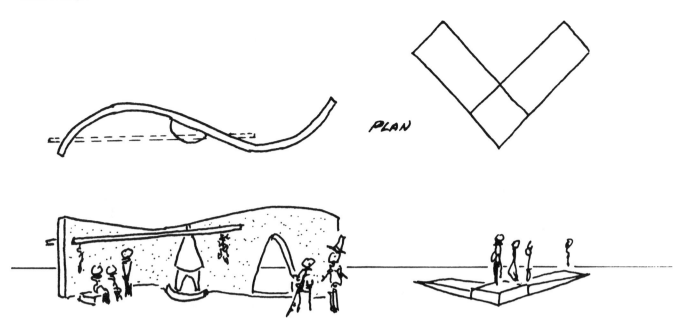

A setting for *Amahl and the Night Visitors* illustrates several of the points already mentioned. The serpentine is one of the oldest of self-supporting forms in architecture. In the second place, the wall "ends" well in space, that is, it does not look incomplete. Third, containment for the interior scene is suggested, without a precise cut-off point. This was an important feature since the chorus of shepherds, a church choral group, was in far greater number than could possibly be contained within the set in a strictly illusionary manner. There is also space for processionals. And, in true sculptural fashion, neither the wall nor the ramp unit leads the eye anywhere but to themselves.

Technically, the serpentine wall rises from 6½' at the concave end to 8' at the convex end, and it is 28 lineal feet long, in seven 4' clamp-together units.

See pages 71-72 for the construction of curved walls; also pages 95-96 for suggestions on simultaneous scenes.

Use of Levels

Ramps, steps and platforms have always been popular in the theatre, and actors can be arranged on them to great advantage. Care must be taken, however, that there is geniune need for levels and that their design is not based on novelty alone. Further, it should be remembered that levels are usually costly to build, are often difficult to handle, and consume great amounts of storage space.

Designers should be aware of certain safety factors when planning for steps and ramps. Interior stairs usually employ 7 or 7½" risers and 10 or 10½" treads (riser plus tread should equal 17 or 17½"). For simplicity, theatre technicians usually go with a 6" x 12" riser-tread combination, which is OK. For very wide treads and low risers, such as in garden design, a good formula is twice the riser plus tread equals 26". As to ramps, none should exceed 1:4 (1' ascent in 4' of run), a pitched acting area should not exceed 1:7, while the Uniform Building Code sets maximum ramp pitch for audiences at 1:8, though most codes use 1:10. 1:4 ramps should be coated with non-slip paint. The methods of construction for steps, ramps and platforms will be found in the Stagecraft II section.

There are five reasons why levels should be attempted, despite all the practical reasons why they should be avoided at all costs!

Visibility

The floor of this cabin for *Sacramento Fifty Miles* has been tipped up primarily in order to add visibility to the loose floor board where the gold nuggets have been stashed away. However, the crooked floor also adds a quality of "wreckiness" to the cabin and motivates the crooked walls and chimney piece which make the cabin appear larger than the 4' x 8' plywood platform upon which it rests. Further details will be found in the Stagecraft II section.

A Level as an Integral Part of the Dramatic Environment

This permanent unit set for the *Barber of Seville* has a balcony attached for the opening scene. The balcony is replaced by an ornamental step and baluster unit for the later interior scenes. Since the window does double duty, the nature of the dramatic action must suggest the inaccessibility of the balcony, which is only 4' above the ground.

Further technical details will be found under platforms in the Stagecraft II section.

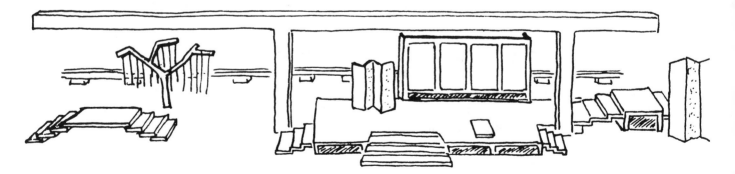

Levels with Assigned Meanings

This single setting for the opera *Butterfly* employs a raised level to indicate the more private areas of Butterfly's house in place of the traditional scene change with illusionary interior. Translucent cloth panels to the rear amplify the emotional states of the actors through suffusion of color and pattern rather than by providing objective scenic detail. Steps are of 4" risers and 16" treads, thus allowing actors to "flow" over them rather than the more usual "stop-and-ascend" action.

Forced Perspective
(cannot be scaled)

Isolation of Environment

A strong platform shape will create a total environment, one that is ideal for space staging. The example shows a triangular platform canted at 9° for a production of *The Dybbuk*. The design intention was to diminish the illusionary force of a nearby proscenium frame. Platform dimensions are 24' across the front, and 20' to the apex, which was 3' above the stage floor. This platform was originally designed for a road tour of *Electra*, and technical details will be found in the Stagecraft II section.

Subdivision of Space for a Complex Play

Elevation
(scale at ¼" = 1')

Shown above is a multiple set piece in the medieval facade tradition designed for Orlin Corey's touring production of *Pilgrim's Progress*. Accessories include tapestries hung before the arches or supported by poles on the deck above, and also curtains, props and backdrops within the facade.

Technical data on this particular set piece will be found in the Stagecraft II section. And the most complete source of information on the traditions and uses of this sort of setting will be found in George Kernodle's magnificent book *From Art to Theatre*.

Profile Exercise

These drawings were made during a workshop at the Arts Lab upon occasion of adding a slab in substitution for the garden archway slab (see cover, also pages 6, 48). All the left sides and the widths are identical. Varying are the dimensions and locations of the arch windows and the top inclines. With a leaded gothic window pane insert, the intention of this slab is to suggest a chapel study. I have placed a small dot in the lower left-hand corner of each of the two slabs I feel are satisfactory. Doubtless there are many other variations as well.

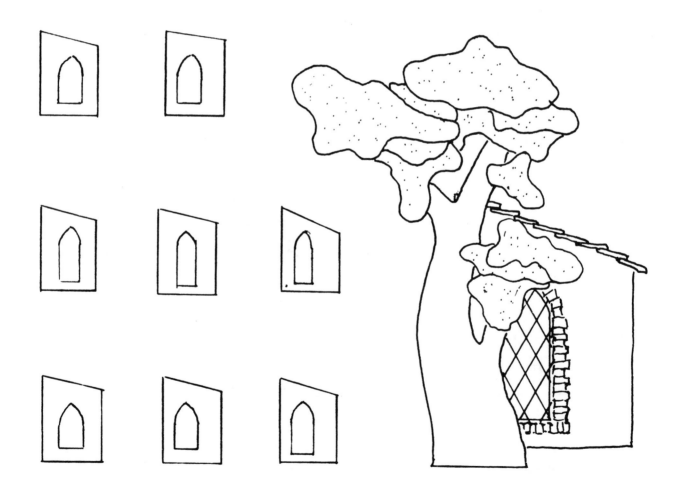

Profile can be a severe taskmaster in the design of self-supporting scenery!

Squares and Quarter Circles

This modular system was initially designed for a creative dramatics program. Once children are shown a few combinations, a seemingly endless number of suggestive environments can be assembled without further supervision. I have found these same pieces invaluable in teaching grown-ups about pure shapes in space plus the necessity for self support.

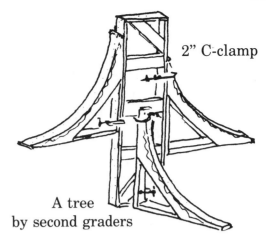

2" C-clamp

A tree
by second graders

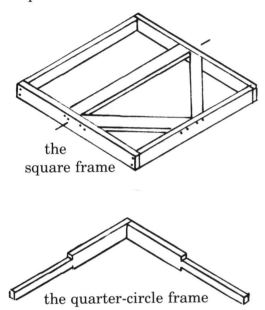

the
square frame

the quarter-circle frame

The **Square** is of "on-edge" construction, measuring precisely 2' x 2'. Make 12 to begin with. The particular layout of clamping strips has proven most effective. Also make a couple of rectangles 1' x 4' as shown in the sketch above.

The **Quarter Circle.**
See also page 19. Since the quarter circle is 2' on a side, the radius of the arc is 23¼". Make six.

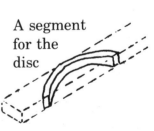

. . . laying out the ¼" ply sweep

A segment
for the
disc

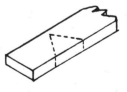

In addition to the above, one needs some battens of various lengths and a number of accessories, such as triangles, discs, etc. The disc shown is 18" in diameter, of ⅜" ply, with clamping segments cut from "2x4" stock. Also inset one clamping batten flush to the rear. A particularly useful device is an adapter by means of which three pieces can be clamped in a 120° configuration to one another. On the table saw, cut three 2' battens and rip a 60° bevel along one side of each. On the band saw, cut two 5" equilateral triangle blocks from "2x6" stock. Notch out as shown and inset the battens flush. All units are undersurfaced and covered on one side only. Use variously colored burlap pieces. Glue burlap on sticks, too.

. . . the 120° adapter block

An interesting "beginner's" design . . .

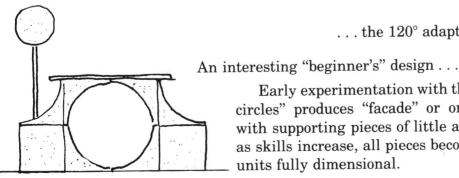

Early experimentation with the "squares and quarter circles" produces "facade" or one-dimensional designs with supporting pieces of little artistic significance. But as skills increase, all pieces become meaningful and the units fully dimensional.

STAGECRAFT II

With freestanding unitary scenery, design and stagecraft are inextricably bound up together, and it is difficult to separate them into compartments. So let's just say that the Design section has been interrupted while we learn some additional techniques which, in turn, may fuel further design options.

Irregular Frames
Framing Up Screens with Top Rails Angled

There are two methods:

1. Assemble stiles, bottom rail and toggles. Lay a measured board across the stiles near the top and parallel to the bottom rail. Establish points (F) and use the diagonal method, as before.

2. Assemble the bottom rail and the longer stile. Using the 18" x 24" framing square for alignment, secure these pieces to the work table. *Screw in* the brace. By this method the fact is recognized that most slope-topped screen panels are the end panels of multiple folds, so that getting the stile that will be hinged at right angles to the bottom rail is all that really matters. Continue with framing up as accurately as possible.

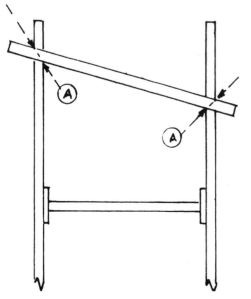

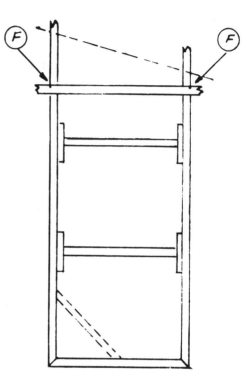

Figuring the Top Angles

If the angle of the slope is unknown, lay a batten across both stiles intersecting the points desired. Mark the intersections of the batten and stiles on both the inner and outer sides as indicated by dashed lines (A) on the drawing to the left. Remove the top rail and turn over. With a straight-edge, connect the intersection marks on the rail and the stiles. Remove both rip and cross-cut guides from the *table* saw and cut by eye. One should have a saw horse the same height as the top of the table saw to help support the assembled frame when cutting the stiles.

If the angle of the slope is known, most cuts can be made with the cross-cut miter gauge on the table saw and prior to assembly. Suppose the angle shown is 15°. Then 7½° are subtracted from 45° for the stile and rail cuts for the joint at the longer stile; and 7½° are added to 45° for the stile and rail cuts for the joint at the shorter stile.

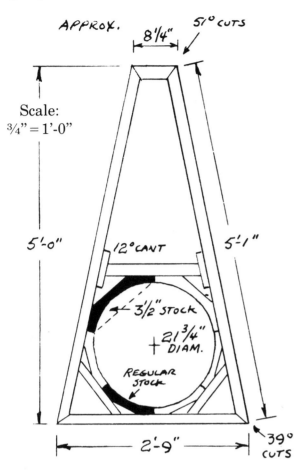

APPROX.

8 1/4"

51° CUTS

Scale:
¾" = 1'-0"

12° CANT

5'-0"

5'-1"

3 1/2" STOCK

21 3/4" DIAM.

REGULAR STOCK

2'-9"

39° CUTS

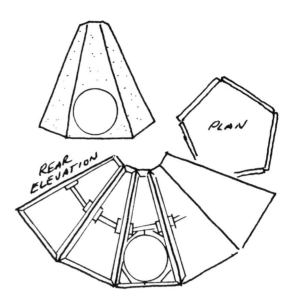

REAR ELEVATION

PLAN

**Framing Up Screens
Non-rectangular in Shape**

A further example of mitered joints is shown by this pentagonal folding screen set for a tepee. Before starting, check to be sure that your cross-cut miter gauge scale registers 90° at center (see page 14). Where so many miter cuts are involved, slight errors have a way of accumulating into whole degrees, so it is suggested that the bottom rails and stiles be cut and assembled first,

then, if the top pieces do not fit perfectly their lengths can be adjusted.

The final covering will prove difficult — beyond imagination! — for a long run of bias edge is involved. The trick is to get the selvage edge down first and then keep the burlap weave at right angles to it by never pulling diagonally as the bias edge is being put down. Incidentally, this is about the smallest hole through which the face burlap can be pulled around to the rear side. (See page 58.)

The tepee is a very popular unit with children. As an abstract shape only, and without permanent decor, it can be a cave, mouse hole, giant metronome, washing machine, steeple clock, piece of cheese, space ship nose cone, trash burner, etc., etc.

35/36" DYED BURLAP & KRAFT PAPER - ECONOMICAL LAYOUT

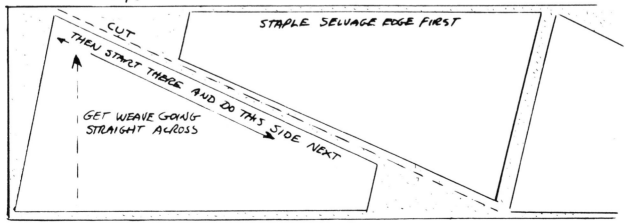

STAPLE SELVAGE EDGE FIRST

CUT

THEN START THERE AND DO THIS SIDE NEXT

GET WEAVE GOING STRAIGHT ACROSS

Plywood Sandwich Technique

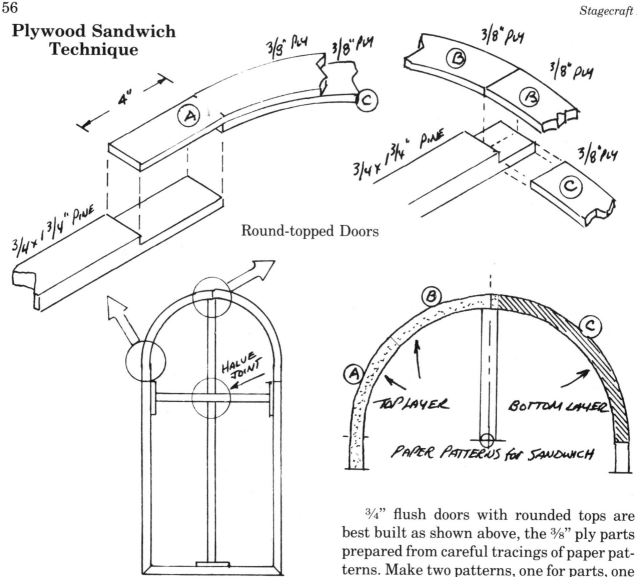

Round-topped Doors

³⁄₄" flush doors with rounded tops are best built as shown above, the ³⁄₈" ply parts prepared from careful tracings of paper patterns. Make two patterns, one for parts, one for assembly guide. Glue and lightly nail overlaps.

Shutters

Shutters are best constructed in three ¼" layers, with ripped pine strips for straightaway framing and ply for curved tops. Stagger joints. In the sketch, right, note that top stile and bottom rail extend to end of frame, locking the corner. Assemble bottom layer over paper pattern, use ½" brads driven flush to hold frame to work table. With white glue, assemble remaining parts, securing temporarily with partially driven 3 penny nails. When set, pry off table and pull ½" brads through or cut off and file smooth.

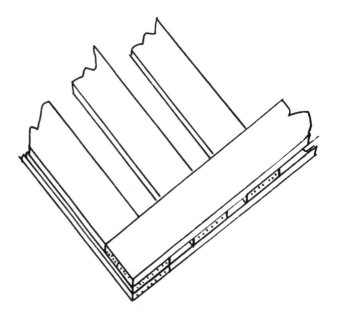

Further Flat-Folding Designs and Techniques

The essential difference between the present edition and previous ones is the organization of the material, in this case, the completion of one useful unit (pages 5-31), and then on into Design, a section that has been much expanded in order to help people stage with unitary scenery.

This approach has of necessity left lots of loose ends, and the Stagecraft II section is where these loose ends are being gathered up. The next several pages continue the subject of flat-folding scenery, including the covering of arch frames, for the manner of covering the arch unit shown on page 31 is not typical of the technique used for strictly modular folding sets.

(See also page 109.)

Modular Screens

On page 24, a modular series of folding arches is shown in serpentine arrangement. It is an example of pure profile, and there is more of a challenge in getting the proportions right than first meets the eye. Note below the distances between the tops of these panels and their arch crowns. It is more important to get the overall proportions right than to satisfy any other requirement.

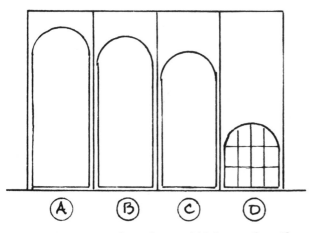

In the examples above, (A) is too fragile, (C) is top heavy, while (B) is well proportioned. (D) obviously suggests a subterra-

nean dungeon beyond, or a fireplace. Thus you can set the dimensions for an archway for an actor to pass through and yet have an unsatisfactory effect. For example, a set of 7'-0" high panels with 6'-3" arch crowns will pass tall actors but will be out of balance aesthetically. On the other hand, these same panels would be suitable for younger actors if the arch crowns were lowered 3".

A Basic Set of Folding Screens?

The question does come up, and there is an answer, if there are no particular reasons for doing otherwise. Remember, this is a far cry from a scene dock filled with standard "flats" because the proscenium frame has "such-and-such" dimensions! But over the years I have found the following sets of folding screens to be most useful, both in themselves and for accessorization, and these are what I recommend for a starter.

For Adult Use

Two sets of plain fourfolds, of panels 2'-9" x 7'-3", one side of *both* sets including lead edges and hinge joints to be of Sea-Rich No. 76 Natural burlap; the other side of one set, No. 124 Eggshell, the other side of the second set, No. 106 Pencil Yellow. Do not confuse Natural with raw burlap. The Natural looks like burlap should look and is worth the "decorator" cost.

One set of threefolds, of panels 2'-9" x 7'-6", with two plain panels flanking one Roman arch panel, crown of arch to be 1'-0" below panel top, to be covered completely with No. 18 Anchor Rust.

One set of threefolds, as above, except that all panels to be arch panels.

One set of gothic arch fivefolds, of panels 2'-6" x 7'-9", crown of arch to be 9" below top of panel, to be covered completely with No. 114 Purple burlap.

Note that where a series of folding arch panels are involved, both sides should be of one color. Note also the slight variations in dimensioning — the arch screens are slightly higher than the plainfolds; the gothic slimmer and higher yet, so that when all screens are involved there will be a proper "balance of parts."

In the sketch above, some arches are "served" by a threefold masking unit. This unit should be lower in height than the arches. If the heights were to be reversed and the masking screen were to overlap the arches, a "proscenium" condition would result, thus countering the space stage working principle of "high point to center." The hallway masking screen on page 40 bears the same relationship to the arch screens there.

For Elementary School Use

For younger people, the heights should be reduced to 5'-9", 6'-0" and 6'-3", respectively, with other dimensions proportionally diminished.

Covering Modular Arch Panels

The method of covering the wall with the arched doorway on page 31 is strictly a custom solution for that situation only and is not typical of the way folding screens are covered with "maximum opening" archway panels. After hinging is completed, these panels are covered from top to a few inches below the arch spring with solid pieces, the sills have fabric attached with white

glue and the stiles are wrapped with strips, ending precisely at the spring lines for symmetry.

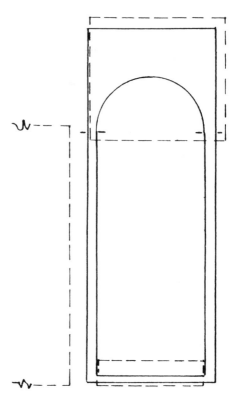

Commence with the solid piece at the top first. Staple the selvage along one side first, cut off any excess and staple along the other side next, following with the top. Tauten the burlap and place temporary holding staples around the arch at 2 or 3" intervals. Leaving about 2" to spare, cut away the excess burlap in the arch area. Slash darts frequently along the curve, but no closer to the arch than ¾". Turn the frame over, pull the fabric up around the curve and staple down. The fabric thus attached represents the "face" or good side of the screen set.

To cover the opposite (secondary) side, the same procedure is followed up to the holding staples, and these are placed a little farther back from the edge of the arch, since the fabric on this side will be tucked under itself about ¹⁄₁₆" back from the edge. Allow about ½" to spare when cutting away the excess fabric in the arch area.

On any curved opening it is important in stapling to skip about here and there rather than working around the opening in one direction so that "fullness" does not pile up. And, of course, without the temporary holding staples this operation would be quite impossible.

On arch frames wider than 33" and where the distance from the top of the frame to the arch spring does not exceed 33" or so, the 35" stock burlap can still be used by turning the roll sideways. This is also the recommended procedure for going around the lead edge of an archway panel at the end of a screen set regardless of width.

The sills of arch screens can be covered with burlap which is secured by white (Elmer's, etc.) glue, which does not stain upon drying. The stiles are covered by strips, commencing along the hinge joint on one side and terminating along the same joint on the other, after being wrapped around the inside of the stile. This strip goes clear to the floor and must be carefully fitted over the half-joint of the sill and stile. Rather than working with precut strips, I use a solid piece, doing one stile at a time. I find the handling easier. Also, I don't have to figure for the extra width when going around a lead stile!

Screen Accessories

In addition to the foregoing "adult" use screen sets, make two single panels, each 2'-9" x 7'-6". Cover one side of each, including the lead edges, with Anchor Rust. Cover the reverse sides with dissimilar colors, perhaps a brightly striped denim on one and a gay color on the other. Set up the threefold which has the one arch panel. Color the archway from the rear with the single panels. There are three color options. Flat

head wood screws through drilled holes in the single panels will secure the panel to the threefold archway.

From some ¾" narrow butts with pins filed down and knocked out, make some loose pin hinges and attach each of the single panels to the threefold as shown in the diagram, bright color facing inward. Coat hanger wire is good for the loose pins. Then a roof piece can be made from refrigerator carton stock as shown on page 4. We call this unit the "sentry box."

With a little ingenuity these same loose pin hinges can also serve in attaching the three-arch threefold unit to the one-arch threefold, for the makings of a hexagonal "pavilion." For more elaborate roof pieces, a "plate" should be added with a curb for the roof piece and a lower cleat which seats itself against the inner face of the panels for stability.

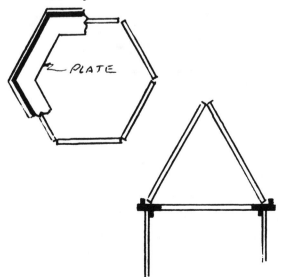

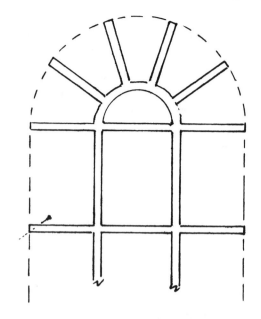

Small finish
nail through
drilled hole

Sketch by
Dan Hanley

With a modular set of folding arches, the making of imaginative inserts for the openings is the name of the game. One of the more useful accessories is a rolling blind such as are hung on verandas. The best way to secure it is by hanging it over a batten which is slightly longer than the blind is wide, having drilled holes for screws at the extreme ends.

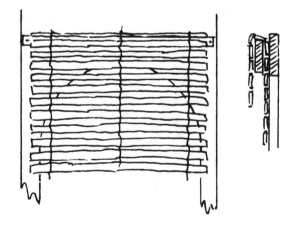

French Window Inserts

Making up room interiors is one of the most practical uses for a series of archway folds. A good example is the drawing room interior for *Let's Make An Opera* found on page 40. *Blythe Spirit* is another play easily done with accessorized archway folds. In the majority of interiors, French windows are essential. Always lay out a full-scale pattern on heavy Kraft paper and proceed as on page 56 with the half joint and ⅜" two-ply sandwich technique. ¾" x 1" muntins are shown in the drawing. There are numerous ways in which the jointing can be executed. French windows are held in place within the archway by small finish nails passing diagonally through drilled holes at the ends of the muntins and on into the edges of the archway stiles.

A Small Puppet Theatre

The theatre can be made easily by accessorizing the three-fold with the single archway.

First we must know the distance from the floor to a few inches above the crook in the elbow of the tallest puppeteer.

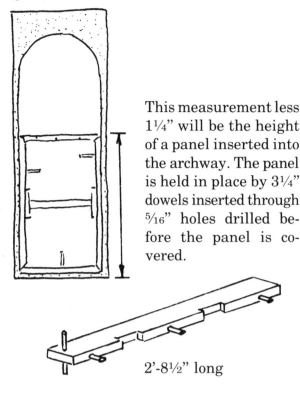

This measurement less 1¼" will be the height of a panel inserted into the archway. The panel is held in place by 3¼" dowels inserted through 5/16" holes drilled before the panel is covered.

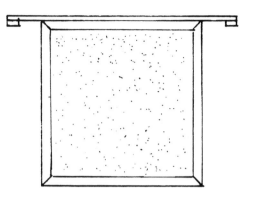

rings, which dictates the nature of the swag. With any tableau curtain, distance (y) must always be greater than distance (x).

2'-8½" long

A wrist board for props, with a dowel for securing the curtain lines and with slots for prop tongues, is set against the rear face of the top rail of the panel insert. To prepare this joint, clamp wrist board in place and drill ¼" holes through the top rail and into the wrist board. Then glue into the wrist board ¼" dowels with ¾" exposed length. Sand exposed dowel portions slightly to fit snugly into rail holes, but not so snug the wrist board cannot be retracted.

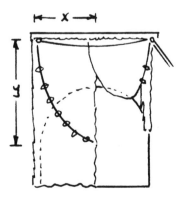

Using jersey cloth, which drapes well, make a curtain that is biparting, tableau rigged, and with 50% fullness pleated to the curtain batten. Notice the pattern of bone

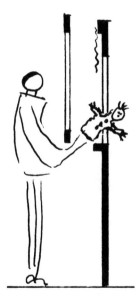

Last is the backcloth which conceals the puppeteers. Maximum visibility for the puppeteers is had by using a framed broadcloth, although a loose curtain can be attached to a batten. The backcloth is placed 10" to the rear of the arch panel, and its bottom should be level with the top of the insert panel. To determine the width, set the flanking panels at 120 degrees to the arch panel and measure in place. A thin strip of wood across the top of the backcloth frame, and somewhat longer, rests upon the tops of the flanking panels.

Wet Process Screen

Adapting "Wet-Process" Muslin Covering to the Flat-Folding System

Painting on burlap and the decoration of already-colored fabrics are arts in themselves and cannot be considered substitutes for traditional scene painting. Yet the question is often asked: "Are there any reasons why sized muslin cannot be used with the self-supporting structural systems described in this book?" Aside from opinion, there are not, *provided* the structures are internally strengthened to withstand the tension when the muslin is tautened by sizing; and *especially,* that the additional and rather time-consuming techniques are mastered when making up the reversible cloth flap hinge for the flat-folding system.

Steps in Making Up A Muslin-Covered Folding Screen

Structure: 3' max. screen width recommended. Toggles every 2'. Not more than 2' of rails unsupported by braces. Belt-sand finished frames.

Fabric Processes: Install 3" edging strips, cut, not ripped, after dipping in thinned white glue solution (equal parts of glue and water). Dip the cut 4" hinge strip in a very weak glue solution (1:4), then staple a small wood block to each end and hang to dry, so as to preshrink hinge strip, to inhibit fraying upon cutting, and to give body to resist paint bleeding. After both edging and hinge strips are dry, place frames to be joined side by side, cut hinges from hinge strip, and mark hinge locations on stiles. Use white glue full strength to attach hinge strips to stiles, being careful not to stick hinges to opposite stile. Carefully separate frames and wipe off any spilled glue. After drying, turn the frames over, carefully pull up hinge strips, push frames tightly together and nail to work table. Attach hinge strips as tightly as possible! Let dry. Remove nails. Fold frames. Commence covering, using thinned glue (1:2). On lead frames, start with selvage along hinge side, ⅛" back from edge. Next do lead edge side, then top and bottom. Trim top and bottom ⅛" back from edges. Carry muslin around lead edge, glue on rear also, and trim. On frames between hinge joints, commence as before, but after setting muslin on opposite side, mark with pencil for ⅛" trim, raise muslin and cut, or trim on inserted cardboard below, then replace muslin. Let dry thoroughly.

Size mulsin in the usual way. When painting, be careful the paint does not dribble down behind the hinge flaps and ruin the other side. Finally, a word of advice. Since the making of muslin-and-glue screens is so time consuming, save those for special uses — intricate decor, repainting needs, wallpapering. Use the ordinary burlap-and-staple screens for plain masking, since a good craftsman can assemble a set of these in four hours or so.

Decor Hinging

The Fabric Hinge As Decor

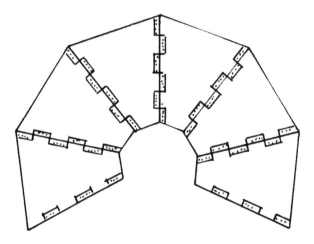

Often it is desired to join panels in this flexible manner which are not to be burlap covered. In such situations the hinge should be regarded as decor and featured with or without an edging strip. One must be neat, turning under the raw edges or overcasting them on a sewing machine set at zigzag. Shown above is a gazebo top made of ³⁄₁₆" Upson board panels. As white glue was used, the cut edges were neither overcast nor turned under. Note the use of false hinge flaps on leading edges to complete the effect.

Show Panels of Fine Fabrics

Folding panels of velour, cut corduroy and velveteen can be made with nearly

Elliptical Arches

invisible fabric hinges and with no staples showing, save along the floor. Paper and cover each frame separately, with the material square pleated at the corners and brought over the top and around the sides, but with the material turned under itself along the bottom. To get the material even and properly taut, commence with a selvage edge on rear face of one stile. Turn frame over, bringing material around. Place temporary staples along the face of the other stile and top rail. Complete finished stapling along the bottom rail. Turn the frame over and complete the stapling along the rear faces of the stile and top rail. Turn the frame over again and remove the temporary staples along the stile and top rail. The dia-

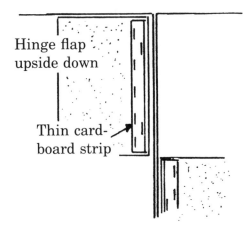

Hinge flap upside down

Thin cardboard strip

gram shows the manner by which the panels are hinged together, with the "blind tacking" upholstery technique. Shown are 4" wide hinges and thin cardboard strips ½" wide. Both the hinges and the cardboard strips should be cut on a standard paper cutter, with the strips being ⅛" shorter than the hinge pieces. Be sure you have the nap of the hinges running the same way as that of the panels themselves. Though the reverse sides of the screens are seldom used due to the different appearance of the backs of the hinges, the reverse sides should be finished in some fashion anyway, for the sake of neatness. Use burlap or some other inexpensive fabric.

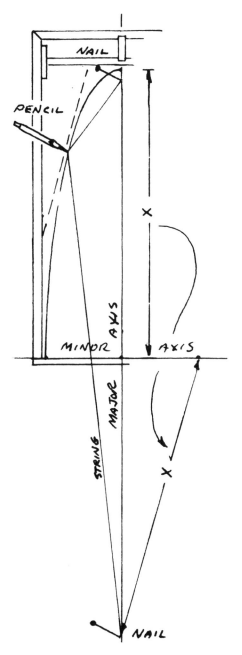

Elliptical arches, being free of historical association possibly because of the difficulty of mounting doors, make wonderfully abstract patterns under the right sort of lighting.

The diagram is self-explanatory. The dashed line is the brace location for folding frames. For slab construction move the dashed line a few inches farther from the arch and prepare a paper pattern of the entire arch sweep for transfer to plywood.

Radial Threefold Screen

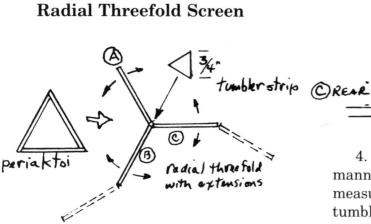

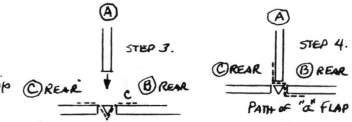

Here is a further application of the reversible cloth-flap hinge used to combine three frames with only one common joint. This doubles the available surface of the three-framed ancient periaktoi.

1. With table saw tilt at 30° cut one triangular tumbler strip of wood the length of the screen height with each face exactly ¾". Glue on burlap.

2. Mask edges of frames to be joined with burlap as usual.

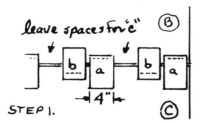

3. Cut a 4" hinging strip. Overcast raw edges with zigzag sewing machine. Then cut strip into 5½" lengths.

4. Join frames. By securing (c) flaps in manner shown in Step 2, exactly 1½" is measured for the "hammock" in which the tumbler strip rests.

5. The purpose of the captive tumbler strip is to maintain tautness of the hinge flaps. When panels are nearly folded, gently rock the pack to and fro in order to permit the tumbler to settle into its proper position. On the negative side, the radial threefold joint is rather mushy, being subject to a greater strain and having double the amount of floating fabric over the regular flap hinge.

(Conceived by Douglas R. Frazier)

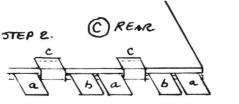

Position of tumbler with screens packed

6. Additional panels can be flap-hinged in the regular manner to any two of the three radials. A limit of one panel to each radial is suggested for reasons given in 5.

Three scenes from
Dickens' *Christmas Carol*

"Dry-brush"
painted decor

Advanced Slab Technique

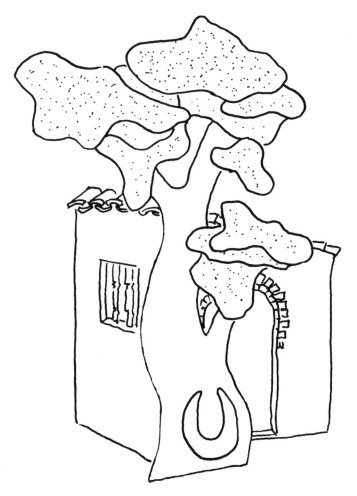

A Slab "T" Joint

Unlike "folding" scenery, slabs can be joined in a variety of ways. The "T" position is the stronger one and preferable to an "L" connection since three rather than two scenes are possible.

Tree design by Irene Corey Barr

Keep slabs as free of permanent detail as possible, accessorizing for specific environments instead. The concept diagram below shows how dimensional "life" can be given a tree without sacrificing compactness. 1-2-3 are the leaf planes, 4 the trunk (these of burlap-covered Upson board) and 5 an offset clamping strip. See page 66 for clamping details.

Tiles are cut from rug roll tubes and mounted on adapter ripped from a 2x4.

Vigas are tubes with wood end discs and are attached by dowel pins.

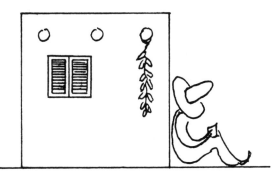

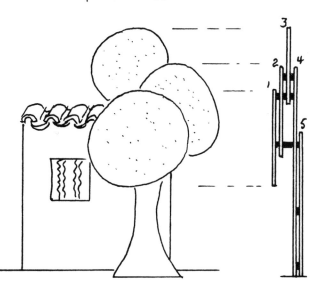

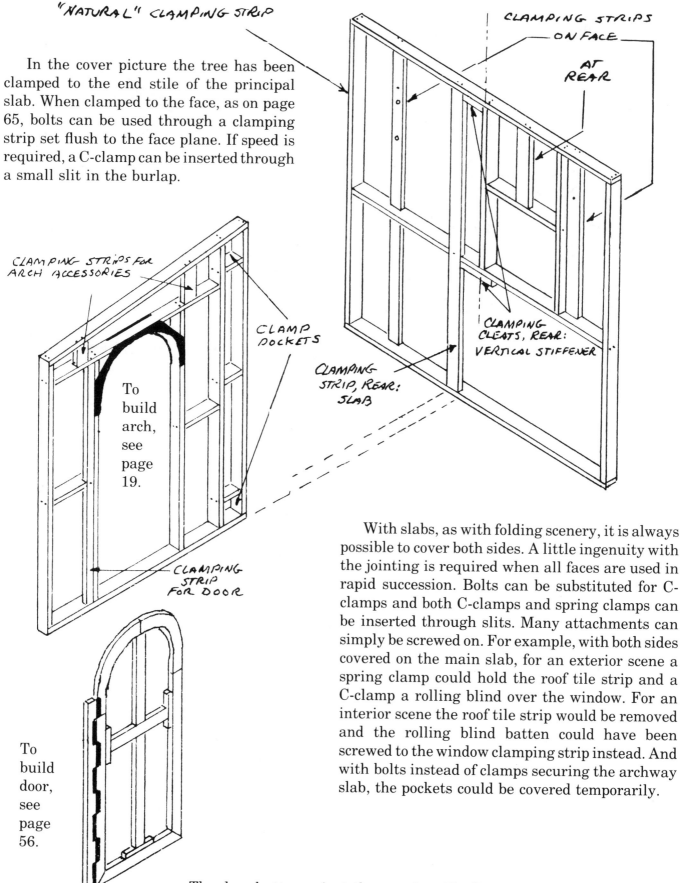

"NATURAL" CLAMPING STRIP

CLAMPING STRIPS
— ON FACE —

AT REAR

In the cover picture the tree has been clamped to the end stile of the principal slab. When clamped to the face, as on page 65, bolts can be used through a clamping strip set flush to the face plane. If speed is required, a C-clamp can be inserted through a small slit in the burlap.

CLAMPING STRIPS FOR ARCH ACCESSORIES

CLAMP POCKETS

To build arch, see page 19.

CLAMPING STRIP, REAR: SLAB

CLAMPING CLEATS, REAR: VERTICAL STIFFENER

CLAMPING STRIP FOR DOOR

To build door, see page 56.

With slabs, as with folding scenery, it is always possible to cover both sides. A little ingenuity with the jointing is required when all faces are used in rapid succession. Bolts can be substituted for C-clamps and both C-clamps and spring clamps can be inserted through slits. Many attachments can simply be screwed on. For example, with both sides covered on the main slab, for an exterior scene a spring clamp could hold the roof tile strip and a C-clamp a rolling blind over the window. For an interior scene the roof tile strip would be removed and the rolling blind batten could have been screwed to the window clamping strip instead. And with bolts instead of clamps securing the archway slab, the pockets could be covered temporarily.

The door butts against the opening. To dimension add ½" to the archway width and from the floor to ¼" above crown.

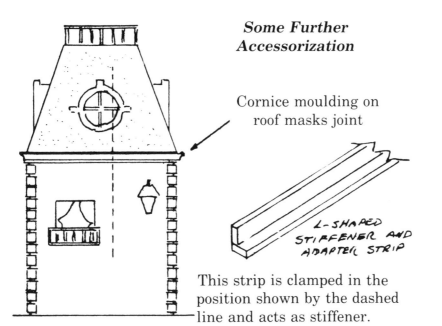

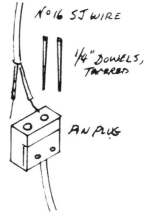

Some Further Accessorization

Cornice moulding on roof masks joint

L-SHAPED STIFFENER AND ADAPTER STRIP

This strip is clamped in the position shown by the dashed line and acts as stiffener.

The burlap covering will camouflage a hole just large enough for the electrical cord from the lamp, but not a connector also, so the bared ends of the wires can be wedged with tapered dowels into the receptacles of a pin plug.

French Town House

The mansard roof is also built with similar "on-edge" construction and lies in the same plane as the supporting slab below. It is further supported by a stiffener, located by the dashed line. The dormer window profiles are established by a change in burlap color. The facing dormer window is cut from ³⁄₈" ply and cloth-backed before attachment. On the slab below, the coigns are small blocks of ³⁄₄" ply, burlap-covered and, for quick change, mounted on L-shaped strips which bolt to the corners. The balcony is dimensional and can be bolted through the window stiles or pinned in the manner of the puppet wrist board, page 61. The lamp is bolted to the clamping/mounting face strip shown on page 66. A clamping strip for the curtain batten is also shown on page 66.

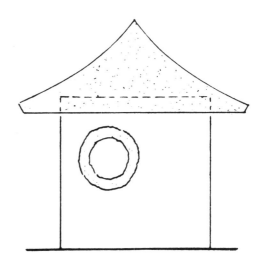

Chinese House

The concave roof, of similar "on-edge" construction, could be clamped to the top of the lower slab, as above, but the overall proportions are improved if the roof slab is dropped somewhat. This is achieved by an L-shaped adapter common both to the roof slab and to the top rail of the lower slab. The offset positioning lends a dimensional effect as well. No vertical stiffener is required. An open disc of ³⁄₈" ply conceals the square window opening.

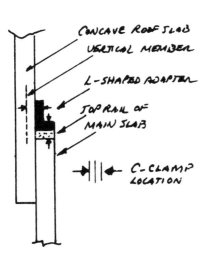

CONCAVE ROOF SLAB
VERTICAL MEMBER
L-SHAPED ADAPTER
TOP RAIL OF MAIN SLAB
C-CLAMP LOCATION

For curved profile construction, see page 70.

MANNEQUIN IN
STORE WINDOW DISPLAY

"IMPROVISATIONS WITH THE CHINESE CASTLE"

The Chinese Castle

Further Combinations
Plus Bent Wood Profiles

The "Chinese Castle" was originally designed as a provocative and
somewhat abstract piece for class work
in improvisations. Among its many ex-
tempore uses were "a castle in a fish
bowl," "a Swiss weather clock," and "a
department store facade with display
window and flanking doors." It has been in *The Mikado* and in numerous Oriental garden
scenes. There are four accessories for the circular opening: a tableau curtain, a wood roll-up
blind, a scrim detailed with the foliage, and a plain cloth for rear shadow projection. There are
also inserts for the archways in the threefold extensions.

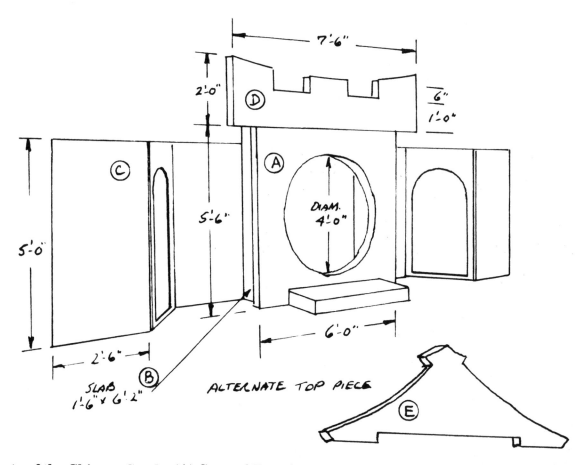

Parts of the Chinese Castle: (A) Central Facade, on-edge; (B) Balance Slab, on-edge, double-
covered; (C) Threefold Screens, flat-framed, with folding strips to clamp to cleats on (B);
(D) Crenellated Parapet, on-edge; and (E) Pagoda Roof Piece, on-edge, to replace (D).

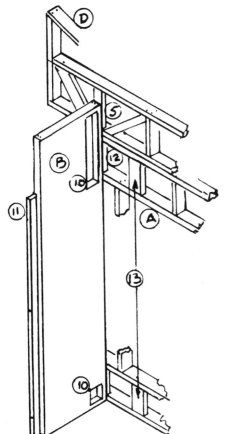

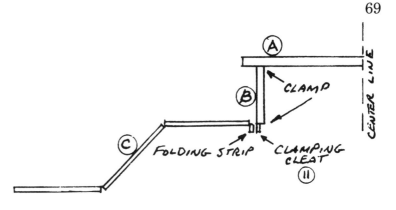

The "Chinese Castle" points up some techniques already suggested and adds some new ones. One point is the use of the balance slab (B) as stiffener to the clamped joint (A-D). Another point of interest is the clamping pockets (10). Slab (B) is exposed to view on both faces, so it must be double-covered. Pockets are structurally framed to a 4" minimum inside clear dimension to accommodate the 2" C-clamps. Then each pocket is opened to the side which is the one more masked from view. Note also clamping cleat (11) on (B) to permit the attachment of the three-fold screen units (C) via a flat-folding strip.

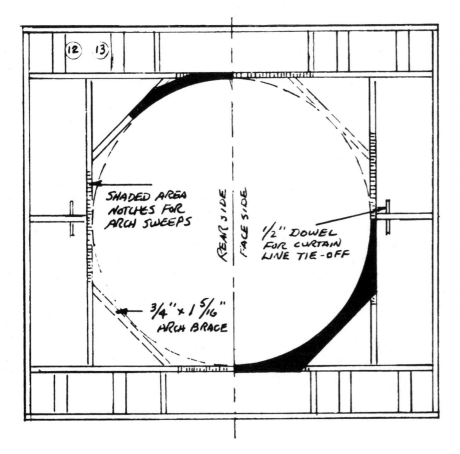

This is the first large arch unit to be built in the on-edge manner, and a considerable amount of ¼" ply will be required for the arch sweeps if they are all cut in quarter-circle segments. I recommend preparing only four of the quarter-circle segments. Set them on one face to get the arch right. Then set in the arch braces. On the opposite face, arch sweeps of one-eighth circle segments can be used at considerable savings.

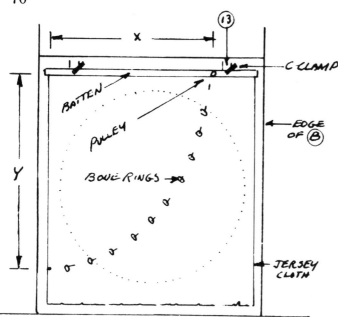

CURTAIN DETAILS

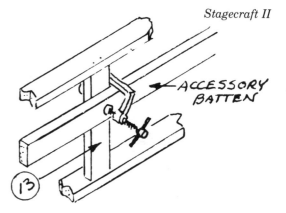

Battens to which accessories are secured, such as curtains, scrims, etc., should be clamped to pieces (13) set vertically to permit adjustment up or down. The C-clamp straddles the battens at a 45° angle.

In setting up a tableau curtain, the contour of the swag is determined by the arc of the rings; also distance "y" must always be greater than "x". Fullness must be from 50% to 100%.

Bent Wood Profiles

Build unit (D) first. Parts are numbered in order of assembly. Assemble through part (6), then clamp in place on (A) and mark braces (7). This will provide a frame rigid enough to prevent tension from (9), a ¾" thick batten ripped down to ½" thick, from warping structure. Parts (8) are marked by temporarily bending in (9) to (6). Excess length is cut off and crenellations removed from (9) after it is secured in place. Note how parts (2) and (6) form stiffeners for the parapet. Unit (E) is triangular in structure and will be harder to get right. After nailing (6) to (1), set on (A) while the (14) parts are plotted *and* secured. (15) is a block of wood acting as a spacer. The (16) pieces are strictly accessories.

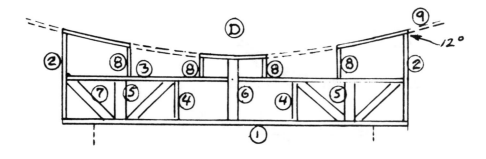

Slab type construction is easily modified to make curved shapes. There are three basic groups: cylinders, cones and spheres.

Cylinders

Segments of cylinders can be made into towers, serpentine walls, fireplaces, etc. Segments of cylinders with long radii also store compactly. The construction of cylindrical shapes is not as difficult as one might imagine, though *absolute precision* must be maintained. Also, the size of the laminated sheets to be bent onto the completed frames should be considered when designing.

For example, using ³⁄₁₆" x 4x8" Upson board laminated cardboard sheets and using the formula C = (pi)(d), you will discover that the widest tower that can be built using one sheet for each of four segments will be 5' in diameter *including* the sheathing.

The first thing to do is to make a full-scale paper pattern as shown at the right below. A B C represents the pattern for the top and bottom sweeps which run through. Trace A B C onto plywood, marking both the positions of the vertical members and A B C positions for later reference. Now cut the pattern up for the A' B' C' pine segments along the dashed lines.

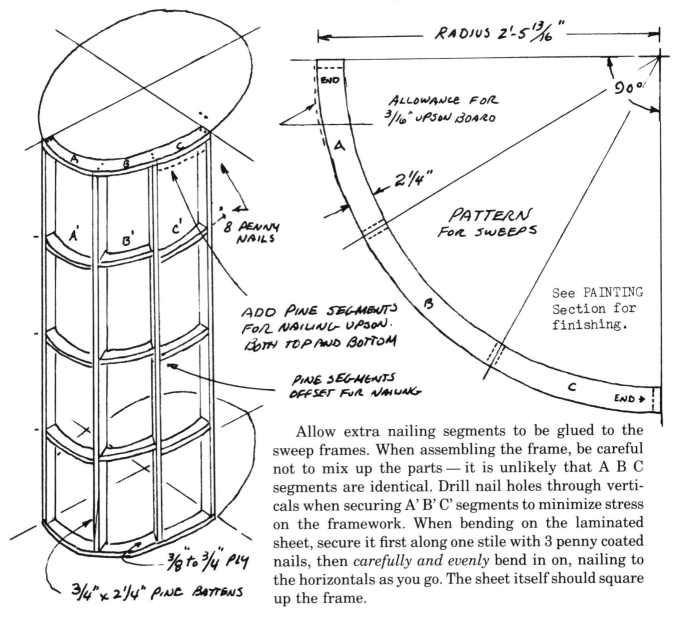

8 PENNY NAILS

ADD PINE SEGMENTS FOR NAILING UPSON. BOTH TOP AND BOTTOM

PINE SEGMENTS OFFSET FOR NAILING

³⁄₈" to ³⁄₄" PLY

³⁄₄" x 2¼" PINE BATTENS

RADIUS 2'-5¹³⁄₁₆"

END

ALLOWANCE FOR ³⁄₁₆" UPSON BOARD

2¼"

90°

PATTERN FOR SWEEPS

See PAINTING Section for finishing.

END →

Allow extra nailing segments to be glued to the sweep frames. When assembling the frame, be careful not to mix up the parts — it is unlikely that A B C segments are identical. Drill nail holes through verticals when securing A' B' C' segments to minimize stress on the framework. When bending on the laminated sheet, secure it first along one stile with 3 penny coated nails, then *carefully and evenly* bend in on, nailing to the horizontals as you go. The sheet itself should square up the frame.

An interesting application of the cylindrical slab shape is the serpentine wall, an inherently self-supporting shape also. Excellent examples of this shape for production are found on pages 37 and 49. The wall shown here consists of five 4' sections with a tapered height from 6½' to 8'. It is faced on both sides with ³⁄₁₆" Upson board, textured with Theatremold, a type of papier maché (see Painting section) and then sprayed. The segments are secured to one another by bolts which are reached by pairs of removable panels of the Upson board about 6" square.

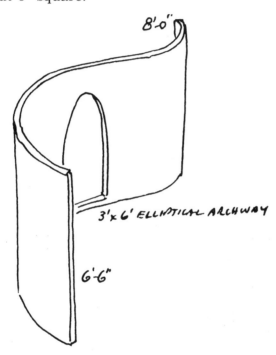

Shown also is the manner of layout. When the curve is reversed, the new radius point must lie along a line drawn from the former point through the juncture point between segments where the curve is to be reversed.

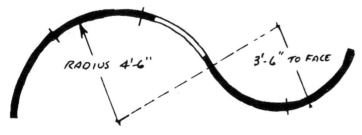

The layout procedure for an elliptical archway is found on page 63. Note the last paragraph. Otherwise, proceed as on page 19 for "on-edge" arch framing. Where very short radii are used, such as in the fireplace in the sketch on page 38, it will be necessary to lay out separate patterns for the front and rear arch sweeps.

Conical Shapes

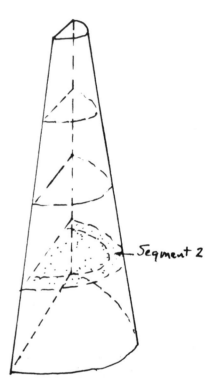

The chimney piece for the fireplace in the cottage sketch on page 38 is an example of one-half of a truncated cone. The base diameter is 3', the height 4', and the angle of taper 15°. On the following page the method of developing patterns for the parts is illustrated. Draw all plans at full scale, of course, so that paper patterns may be cut out for tracing. Do the section first. In order to simplify calculations, negotiate the 4' x 4' (+) or (−). In the drawing,

I am using ½" ply for the horizontal segments, with 11" between them. The drawing also shows how the horizontal segments are developed. Set the band saw table tilt to 15° when cutting the arcs of these segments. The 2½" width of parts, also the thickness of the ply, is arbitrary. ⅜" ply would be OK, but the calculations would be

Spheres

Spheres are developed in much the same manner, the vertical segments being curved also. The teapot shown is 3' in diameter, with horizontal segments every 6". The teapot was surfaced with narrow strips of cardboard, after which cheesecloth that had been dipped in wheat paste was applied and pressed down as smoothly as possible.

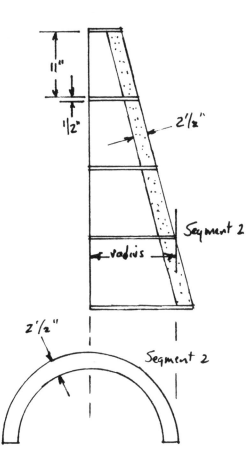

more difficult. If you should ever have to build a complete cone, the verticals must end as shown, and the point itself would have to be cut from a solid block of wood.

At right is a partial sketch showing how the vertical segments are staggered for easy assembly.

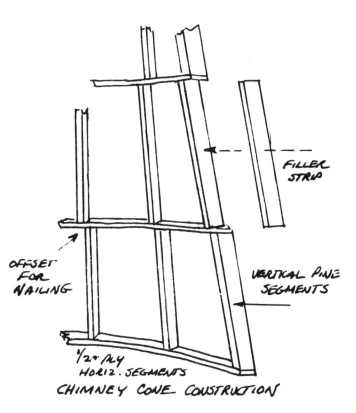

CHIMNEY CONE CONSTRUCTION

Platforms, Steps and Ramps

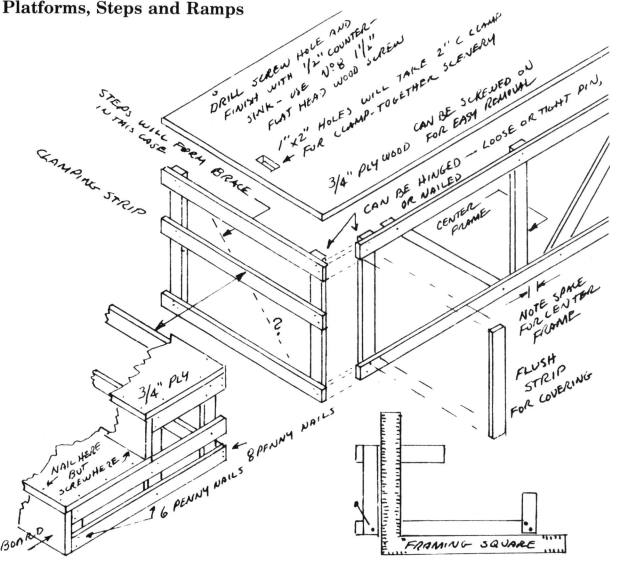

DRILL SCREW HOLE AND FINISH WITH 1/2" COUNTER-SINK - USE N°8 1½" FLAT HEAD WOOD SCREW

STEPS WILL FORM BRACE IN THIS CASE

1"x2" HOLES WILL TAKE 2" C CLAMP FOR CLAMP-TOGETHER SCENERY

3/4" PLYWOOD CAN BE SCREWED ON FOR EASY REMOVAL

CAN BE HINGED — LOOSE OR TIGHT PIN,

CLAMPING STRIP

CENTER FRAME

NOTE SPACE FOR CENTER FRAME

FLUSH STRIP FOR COVERING

3/4" PLY

NAIL HERE BUT SCREW HERE

8 PENNY NAILS

16 PENNY NAILS

BOARD

FRAMING SQUARE

Lap-Joint Construction
using standard ¾" x 1¹³⁄₁₆" stock
Scale: 1" = 1'-0"

This system is appropriate for high platforms, for platforms which must be disassembled, and for most straight-run steps. Basic "framing-up" technique is discussed on the following page. Here, note particularly the use of a pine board riser and a plywood tread. Plywood is selected for the tread because it is stronger and can be deeper than a pine board whose width seldom exceeds 11½". Pine is selected for the riser since it will be nailed (or screwed) into. When the width of a step unit exceeds 2', add an inside frame, up to three inside frames for a tread 8' wide, this being the widest practical dimension as most plywood comes in 4x8' sheets.

For the same reason, platform units seldom exceed 4' x 8'. For larger platforms, clamp units together. Add center frames for each 2' of platform length, likewise. Since platforms, unlike steps, are usually disassembled, the inside frames need not be attached, but may rest between cleats, as they provide support only to the platform tops. When joining outside platform frames by hinging, all hinges should be at the inside corners in order to make the unit as rigid as possible. For disassembly, use loose pin hinges in one pair of corners diagonally opposite each other.

After all the necessary inner parts have been added, pry up the frame from the table, turn the frame over, and turn down the ends of the nails with the hammer.

6 PENNY LIGHT BOX
CEMENT COATED NAILS

3/4"

FRAMING SQUARE

Starting a Lap-Jointed Frame for a Platform

The large diagram shows the perimeter parts for a frame which will form one long side of a platform 2' high and 6' long. On the work table, place the two rails (A) and (B), each cut to 6'. Lay on top of them the two stiles (C) and (D), cut 1'-11¼" long (assuming a ¾" ply top). (C) and (D) will be offset ¾" from the ends of (A) and (B) to permit end frames to be joined (see insert diagram). Hammer all the way in one 6 penny coated nail to join (C) to (A). This nail will also lock this joint to the work table, hence the need for the soft pine or spruce top as specified on page 9. Now nail (D) to (A). This locks (A) to the table completely. With the framing square, align (D) to (A) and hammer in the second 6 penny nail. Move the framing square to the other end and repeat this operation. Now adjust (B) to (C) and (D) and place one 6 penny nail at each joint, and don't hammer the nail all the way down into the work table yet, but check these joints for "square." If something is way out of line, recheck the lineal measurements of all parts, then use the diagonal squaring up method as explained on page 21. When the frame is rectangular, complete joints (B-C) and (B-D), then add the second nails.

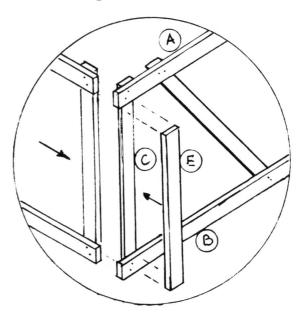

It is always best to have the long framing members on the outside, thus, for covering purposes, short battens (E) can be inserted between the long sides and over the shorter parts, such as (E) over (C) and between (A) and (B), offset, of course, so the corner is flushed up completely.

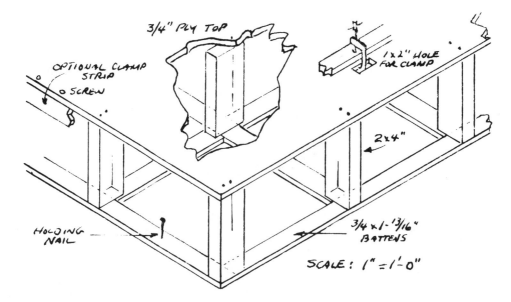

The Stud System

This system applies to low level platforms, ramps, and double-tilted platforms. The system involves the use of short "studs" (usually up to 24" or so) between a sole plate frame and plywood decking. Proper support comes from the frequency of the studs themselves since the platform top is not ribbed. Scrap ends of 2x4s and 2x6s are useful here. The drawing above shows how the proper placement of each stud interlocks the structural members of the plate frame itself.

To construct a level platform, subtract 1½" from the overall height, cut the studs, then secure decking to studs first. Now turn over and add the plate members. No further bracing is necessary.

To construct a ramp, make a large-scale drawing so that the angle of rise can be accurately determined by a protractor. Then make the end cuts on the plywood decking as shown by the detailed drawings below. For the flat cut, an auxiliary guide made of an L-shaped wood strip will provide a guide which can be set tight against the saw blade. For the vertical cut, use the rip guide alone, and necessary gap between blade and guide will blunt somewhat what would otherwise be a too delicate "feathered" edge.

Continue by figuring the studs at the high end first, and after notching for the rib clamping cleat, set these studs, then figure the remaining studs by measuring in place. Secure all side studs, then turn the ramp over and attach the side plate strips, add cross plate strips and central studs.

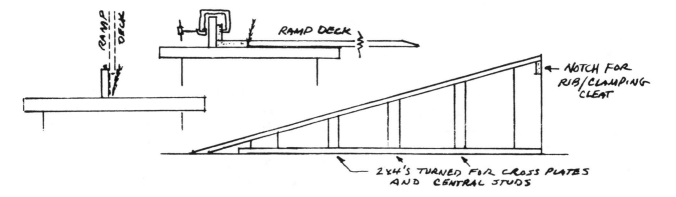

With double-angled platforms, set the studs at the four corners first. Stud cuts will require compound miters at one end, that is, with both the miter gauge and the blade tilt. The illustration shows the platform for the *Sacramento Fifty Miles* cabin as drawn on page 50.

"Clampatibilty"

A giant plus for both systems of platform construction is the natural compatibility with the slab type construction through clamping. An excellent example of multiple structural interlocking is the *Barber of Seville* unitary set shown on page 50 and in the accompanying sketches on this page. Lap-framed platform (F) is first set up, then slab-framed stiffeners (G) are clamped on.

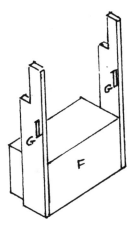

On the face of (F-G) the slab units (A-B-D-E) are clamped on as well as clamped to each other. (C) units are attached to (A-B) and made rigid horizontally by a stiffener (not shown) which passes through the slots in the (G) units. On page 50, a balcony unit is shown for the opening scene. On this page is shown the ornamental step-and-baluster unit which has been substituted for the interior scenes.

Always a Problem

Steps and platforms have always been a structural challenge to the theatre technician. Systems devised for proscenium stage use exclusively take for granted (1) soft wood floors for accessory stabilization, (2) ample off-stage space for more solid units, usually castered, and (3) veneer facing rather than facing that is integral to the platform system. And the popularity of overall floor elevations of one sort or another in recent years has led to a variety of solutions most of which are good only for the "run of the production" and salvaged thereafter.

No system of elevations other than the traditional "parallel" and the "stringer" step unit can lay claim both to flexibility in handling during production and compactness in storage, but these units have the dual problems of integral stability and facing.

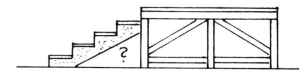

Shown above is a typical stringer step unit and parallel platform. The idea behind the "parallel" is that once the top, cleated on the underside to prevent slippage, is removed, the frame can be collapsed flat by a special arrangement of hinges. The problems are that the top creaks and the "parallel" is always trying to fold, and remedies to prevent these problems defeat the flexibility of the unit. The idea behind the stringer step unit is its compact nature, it being cleverly cleated onto the parallel frame, but when the "?" area is solved, either you have another piece of scenery or the loss of the compactness. Neither unit is particularly suitable for space staging.

Thus, with the exclusion of these units, platforming in general is pretty much a matter of custom solutions for conditions at hand. The lap-joint method of platform construction previously described is inherently stronger than "parallels," and units do store well when disassembled. While lap-jointed step units don't come apart, they can carry

permanent facing and are extremely rigid, lending further stability to platforms to which they are clamped. The stud method makes for stability also, and these platforms and ramps are easily faced, though they must be stored intact.

A traditional method of getting up platforms for one-shot custom deals is ribbing them with 1x4s (though some timid souls go to 2x4s), and then adding vertical posts, bracing where necessary. This is often referred to as the "kitchen table" solution — for nothing lines up, though the elevation is accomplished without much forethought, or foresight, as the case may be.

There are two variants of this method which have appeal for space-stagers on tour. The first is the use of heavy pipe with flanges for legs in conjunction with the ribbed platform tops. This system has the advantage of adjustable heights by pipe

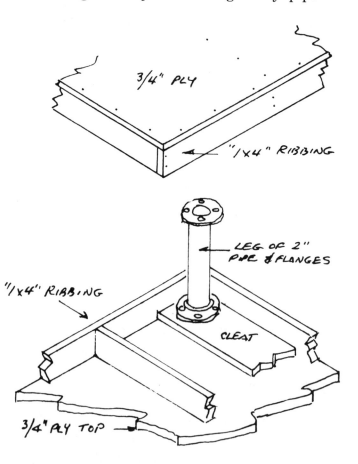

length interchange. Also, platform overlaps are possible where space is short. One should carry plenty of shims, though, for pipes and pipe flanges seldom thread up uniformly. (See also the Lighting section for the making up of spotlight stands using pipes and flanges.)

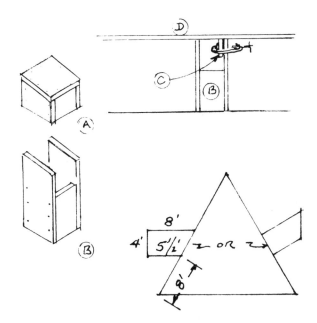

The other variant is to clamp box-like legs to the underside of ribbed platform tops. This is a particularly good solution if a large ramped platform is involved, such as that shown on page 51.

A diagram shows how the platform units are arranged. The 24' dimension rests along the stage floor and the platform slopes upwards at about 9°. Assembly begins with the three front platforms with their rear edges balanced on the appropriate (A) legs. Then the (B) legs are clamped to the ribs. Since the (A) legs must level the joints, they cannot be clamped in the same manner, so a clamp is set against each one to prevent its slipping upstage. And the platform units are, of course, clamped to one another as well.

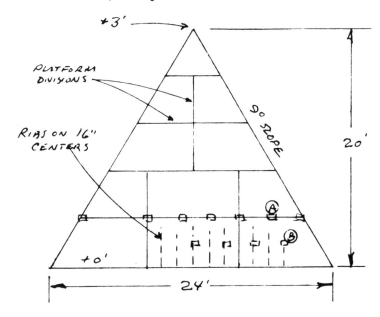

Access ramps are difficult to figure because compound angles are involved. For example, the particular access ramp shown will fit only as laid out on the little plan and cannot be relocated either farther up or farther down, unless, of course, the end angle is changed. A quick way to do this figuring is to erect that portion of the platform involved on the work table and then connect the ramp piece, as yet uncut, to the platform at the desired location, letting the ramp piece hang over the edge of the work table. Then move the platform around until the ramp piece lies flat along the work table edge. Draw the desired line with a pencil on the underside of the ramp piece, disassemble, and cut the ramp piece. Ramps should be supported by the stud method.

Circular Stairs

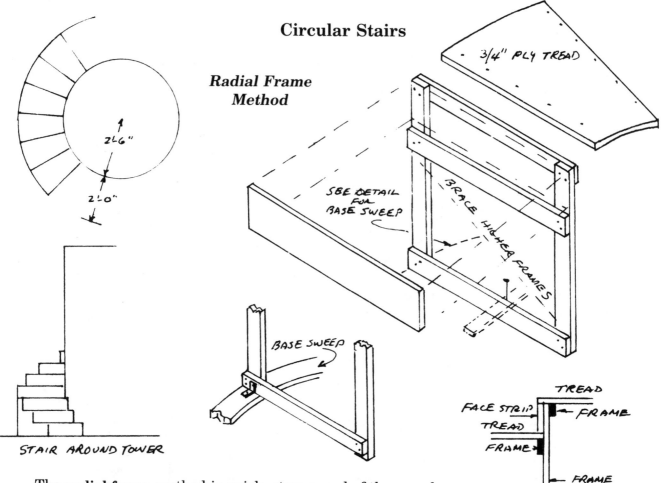

Radial Frame Method

3/4" PLY TREAD

SEE DETAIL FOR BASE SWEEP

BRACE HIGHER FRAMES

BASE SWEEP

STAIR AROUND TOWER

2'-6"

2'-0"

TREAD
FACE STRIP — FRAME
TREAD
FRAME
FRAME
FRAME — EITHER SIDE

The **radial frame** method is quick, strong, and of the easy lap-joint construction. This method produces a smooth curve, but the stairs must be faced with a veneer such as Masonite or Upson board. Since stairs by this method cannot easily be stored, divide the total run into segments, perhaps a half dozen steps at a time, and these segments can be stacked tread to tread to save some space. Note particularly how a base sweep is inserted in order to provide for the nailing of the veneer along the bottom.

Pier Method

The **pier** method is similar in appearance to the radial frame method, but is conceived of as a series of vertical shafts each of which carries a separate tread. Details are found on the following page. The elevations shown here refer to the lower illustration on page 51.

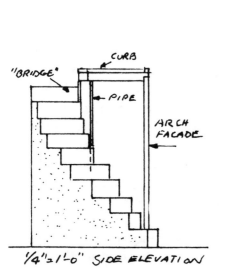

CURB
"BRIDGE"
PIPE
ARCH FACADE

1/4"=1'-0" SIDE ELEVATION

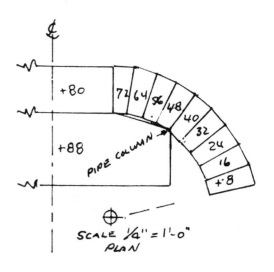

+80   72 64 56 48
           40
+88 PIPE COLUMN 32
                  24
                  16
                  +8

SCALE 1/4"=1'-0"
PLAN

Circular Stairs — Pier Method

Here is truly a breakthrough in circular stair design for those who face stiff transport and storage requirements. Furthermore, these stairs are so sturdy that considerable support is transferred to any scenery that is clamped to them.

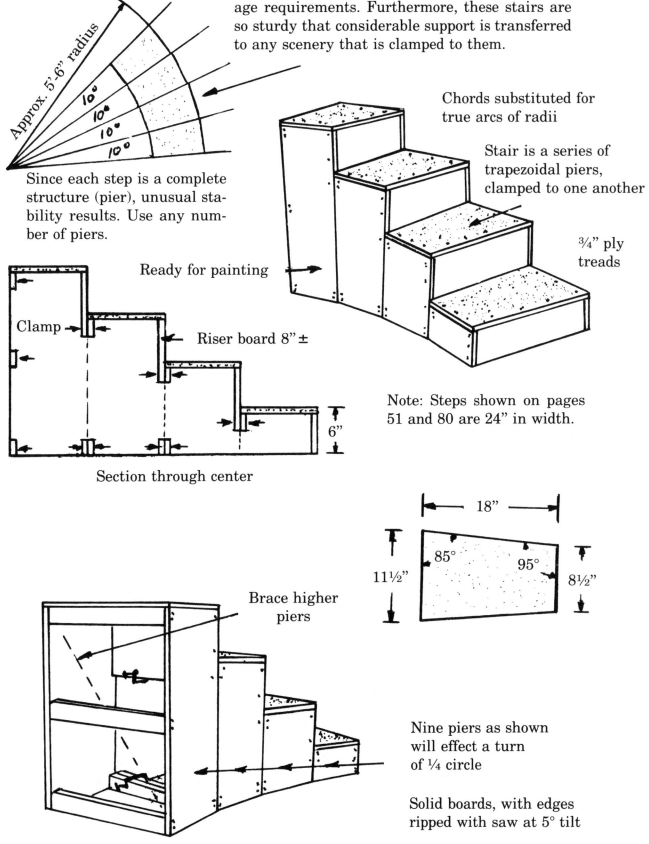

Approx. 5'-6" radius

10° 10° 10° 10°

Since each step is a complete structure (pier), unusual stability results. Use any number of piers.

Chords substituted for true arcs of radii

Stair is a series of trapezoidal piers, clamped to one another

¾" ply treads

Ready for painting

Clamp

Riser board 8" ±

6"

Section through center

Note: Steps shown on pages 51 and 80 are 24" in width.

Brace higher piers

18"

11½"   85°   95°   8½"

Nine piers as shown will effect a turn of ¼ circle

Solid boards, with edges ripped with saw at 5° tilt

Furniture

It is necessary to construct a considerable amount of furniture for the space stage for the simple reason that most "borrowed" furniture is too large for it, even with many "grown-up" sized sets. Space staging always suggests a lesser scale than reality. Besides, furniture made in the stagecraft shop along with the freestanding scenery creates a better sense of reality.

It is important to note that the same does *not* hold true for the literal illusion created by the conventional "interior" box set of flats. There, actual period furniture appears to advantage. As has been stated before, the concepts and practices advanced in this book and those of the proscenium discipline are neither compatible nor interchangeable.

All furniture depends on craftsworthy **jointing** and proper **framing** where applicable. It is obvious that without the ability to cut and rip easily at prescribed angles, the fabrication of most of these pieces would become both difficult and time-consuming.

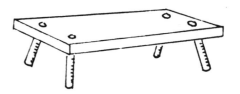

An example of simple jointing is the small stool or bench, consisting of a seat of 2" stock (1½") drilled for 1" dowels for legs. Cut dowels to length on table saw with the angle desired set on the miter gauge. Sand ends of dowels lightly to create chamfered edges which will prevent splintering. Rub white glue on legs and inside holes. Set legs in place with hard rubber mallet. After glue has dried, sand top smooth.

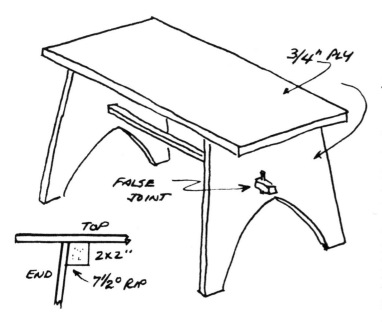

An example of framing is the refectory table. The ends and top comprise the basic frames. The joints common to top and ends are strengthened by lengths of 2" x 2" angle ripped to 7½° along one side. The stretcher (2" x 3" suggested) with 7½° cuts must be carefully fitted. Secure ends to stretcher with #9 flat head wood screws 2" long. Then add false ends as sketched for the illusion of a medieval fitted and pegged joint. If the table is over 4' long, a center board is suggested parallel to the stretcher and secured to the underside of the top between the ends.

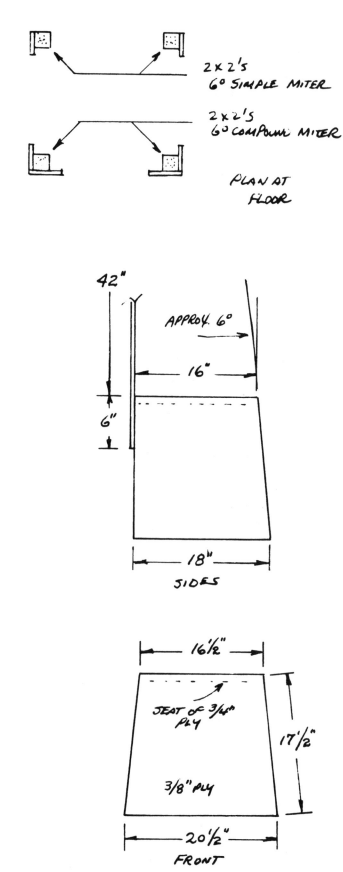

2 x 2's
6° SIMPLE MITER

2 x 2's
6° COMPOUND MITER

PLAN AT
FLOOR

42"

APPROX. 6°

16"

6"

18"

SIDES

16½"

SEAT OF ¾"
PLY

17½"

3/8" PLY

20½"

FRONT

2x2"

The court chair illustrates a useful rule of stage furniture design: "Keep the fancy decor where the structure isn't!" With this in mind, the chair becomes a box with two of the six sides missing. After the scrollwork is done, assemble the seat and three sides, using 3 penny coated nails carefully aimed. Then add the vertical 2x2s along the inside corners as shown on the floor plan. Before the back is attached it should be strengthened by a tapered batten running down the rear centerline — say 46" long and tapered from ½" near the top to 1¾" at the bottom.

A good exercise in cutting both simple and compound miters is had in the two versions of the stool at right. 2x10" squared tops and 2x2s for legs and stretchers are employed.

By fabricating stage furniture with care so that it will last for many years, and by following the simplest and most universal designs, in a relatively short time a "saturation" point will be reached where the piece will more likely exist than have to be made from scratch.

The legs for stool A are cut with compound miters; that is, the blade is tipped at 7½° and the miter gauge is set 7½° off 90°. The stretchers are cut with a simple miter, the 7½° taken either by the blade tilt or the miter gauge, but not both.

The legs for stool B, set catty-cornered, also the cross stretchers, are cut at a simple miter of approximately 10½° (to maintain the same *effective* angle of slope, 7½° must be multiplied by the factor 1.414). Large nails (20 penny, common, bright) are used to secure all joints, with passing holes drilled through the first members of the joints. The crossed stretchers pass by means of the half joint.

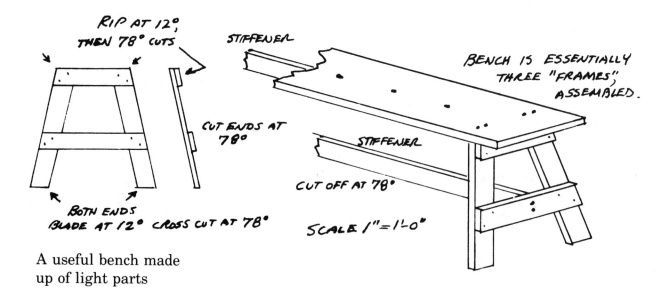

A useful bench made up of light parts

Lanterns and Lamps

For larger lamp fixtures, such as the pirate ship-type lamp at left, one needs a porcelain socket, medium-screw, a tubular frosted "show-case" or orchestra stand lamp, and frost color medium preferably plastic. Of the latter, a large tube can be formed and gelatine color such as orange or amber inserted in it, and the whole unit placed over the frosted tubular lamp to spread the glow. It is also imperative to cover the openings of the fixture on the interior side with a fine quality cloth such as a man's white shirt fabric so that the flow of light appears more evenly distributed.

Sources of illumination on stage are essential to night scenes. One does not indicate night or dark effectively merely by lowering the intensity of the acting lights only, but by the contrast which is built up between scenic lamp fixtures, translucent window panels and hand lanterns *and* the level of the general lighting.

Porcelain socket

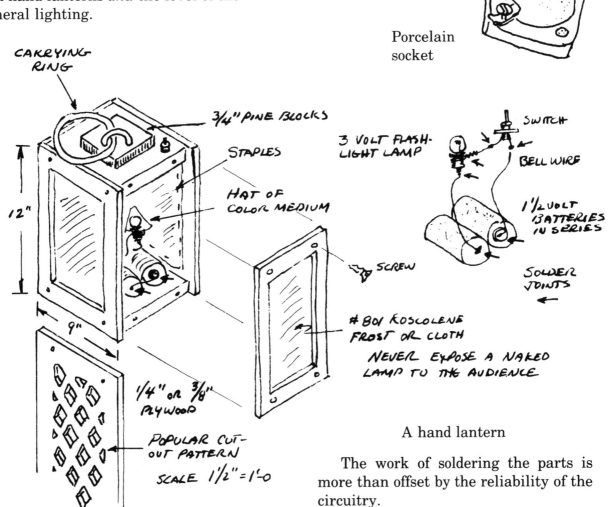

A hand lantern

The work of soldering the parts is more than offset by the reliability of the circuitry.

SCENE PAINTING

This section is devoted to permanent painting of a highly suggestive nature on dyed, textured fabrics. As has been pointed out in this book, the need for painting at all is an occasional one and entirely optional on the part of the designer. In fact, it was many years before I used any decoration other than the dyed materials themselves plus custom accessories. Later on, I worked with shading by spray gun, and, finally, I reached the conclusion that there were certain types of scenery and imagery which could be painted in detail and used over and over again. If a change of painted detail were necessary, the fabric was unstapled and saved, and a fresh fabric stapled down. I also realized that detailed imagery on a frankly modular folding screen should taper off before reaching the edges of the panels, and, of course, a dyed fabric base is essential here.

But invariably the question comes up, "Why can't we do all this in muslin, for painting and repainting?" I think the reasons we don't are fairly obvious, but for one thing, our system of framing is not strong enough to withstand the tautening up of any large areas of muslin. It was never

intended to be for reasons of portability and use by children. And for another, I believe

the quality of a dyed, textured fabric is fundamental for space-oriented scenery, and this is lost by complete color coating. For still another reason, the folding screen joint becomes somewhat of a nightmare when muslin and glue are substituted (see pages 61-62). And after several repaintings, what then? Washing may unseat the joint strips . . .

Paint

With textured fabrics, both plain and dyed, there is really no type of paint which cannot be used. Rather, it is a matter of how the paint is applied. Remember that a solid color covering coat cannot be applied by brush, since the texture fills up, the fabric loses its tension and a very unattractive surface results.

Yet there are times when a fabric of a desired dye is unavailable, or when faded burlap must be restored, or when raw burlap is used and a solid color is required. Then, paint should be sprayed on as lightly as possible. Short of this, a very soupy mixture of paint can be hand-rubbed in, using an absorbent cloth or sponge in order that all paint may be removed in excess of that required to stain the fibers.

For additional texturing and the detailing of the more literal imagery by brush, I prefer acrylic latex paints. Locally one can get by with a gallon of exterior tinting white house paint and some artists brushing powders including bright red, magenta, orange, medium green, ultramarine blue and chrome yellow — also some black paint. If you have a stock of dry scenic color pigments already, use with the acrylic latex white for tinting and binding in lieu of the whiting and glue. Better still, some scenic houses now stock acrylic stage paint. Write the Olesen Co., 1535 Ivar Ave., Hollywood, CA

90028, for a catalog and a color card. Purchase one gallon of white and the following quarts for a good stock: magenta, fire red, thalo dark green, acacia yellow, venetian red, burnt sienna, raw sienna, black, thalo bright red, and ultramarine blue.

Brushes

Four brushes are required:

1 — 1" scenic liner
1 — 2" scenic liner
Preferably of white imported bristle and usually available from scenic supply houses. I have purchased both from the Alcone Co., 32 West 20th St., New York, NY 10011, and the Olesen Co., 1535 Ivar Ave., Hollywood, CA 90028. These are expensive, but there are no substitutes.

1 — No. 6 Pointed Brown Hair Bamboo brush, available from most commercial art stores, or from Dick Blick, P.O. Box 1267, Galesburg, IL 61401.

1 — 1½" very worn out, stubby, ordinary paint brush.

Miscellaneous

Flat pie tins (cheap dime-store aluminum ones OK) for three purposes: brush can be dipped on its side, brush can be wiped off flat and evenly, and tin can be used as mixing palette.

Muffin tins for mixing colors.

White chalk for sketching.

Pastel chalks and cray-pas for detail and shading.

Can of clear plastic spray to fix pastel chalks and any colors not put on with waterproof binder.

Detailing by Paint — Brushwork
(Notes by Irene Corey)

Burlap lends itself beautifully to detail painting. The small fibers which extend upward from the surface of the cloth catch the light and create a soft, rich effect. In a simi-

lar manner, these fibers catch the paint, leaving the basic color underneath as contrast. Virtually any scenic effect can be achieved on burlap by the "dry-brush" technique so long as the basic color of the burlap selected is a medium value tone so that both highlight and shadow colors will contrast with it. "Dry-brush" as used here is a technical term in which as little liquid is used on the brush as is necessary to deposit the pigment on the outer nap only. The paint must be of a thick, heavy cream consistency, such as that of acrylic latex as it comes from the can. When several colors are dry-brushed in the same area, the result is a rich hue, the colors blending in the beholder's eye in the manner of Impressionist painting.

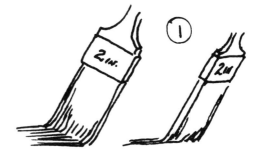

Illus. 1: "The liner is the most useful of the brushes, for by it both wide and thin strokes are made . . ."

Painting Techniques
Plaster Walls and Bricks (Illus. 3)

For plaster walls on natural burlap, make the highlighted areas, suggesting slightly raised portions of the plaster, with the 2" liner, dipped in creamy beige paint. Hold the brush at about 30° and glide onto and off of the surface in much the same way as an airplane pilot practices continuous landings and take-offs, thus creating feather edges. Every effort must be made to keep the paint on the outer fibers of the burlap only, avoiding complete saturation. Strokes can go in many directions.

Develop highlights further by changing pressure during the stroke or varying the amount of paint on the brush. Shadowing is done the same way as highlighting, using bluish brown. Areas where the plaster has peeled away are also shadowed. Lath below plaster will cause the plaster to be stained brown. Bricks produce an orange stain. Complete the detailing by marking a greater portion of the crack line with brown with the lining brush, then shading away from this line with bluish white. Learn how to do only a portion of the plaster wall in complete detail, and continue by highlighting and shadowing beyond this area, ever less prescisely. In this manner the majority of the surface need not be detailed, but is suggested. Finish by lightly brushing a trace of yellow across some of the highlighting.

Bricks are made with the 2" flat lining brush using wide strokes. Make each brick length with one stroke only! Wider bricks may require two stroke-lengths. Start with dark orange-red or brown. Mix white into the brick tones. Accent with bright orange or pink-orange. Allow some bricks to fade away as if still covered with plaster. Lay in bricks in plastered areas to suggest they have "bled" through by mixing white into the brick tones. For mortar between bricks, shadow with dark blue gray, using the 1" liner. *Do not outline* more than a few of the bricks, but merely suggest the mortar occasionally.

Adding Vines and Leaves (Illus. 2 & 4)

For vines, hold the 1" lining brush nearly perpendicular to the painting surface with the narrow side leading. Use greens and browns. Let the ends of the vine trail away to nothing. For leaves, start the 1" lining brush moving sideways to make a thin line. Press down on the brush and also rotate slightly for the flat part of the leaf. Return to the thin line position. Use the pointed hair brush for small details such as leaf veins or highlights and shadows. A slight touch of yellow will often make the leaf appear more life-like. Always move the brush in the direction things grow.

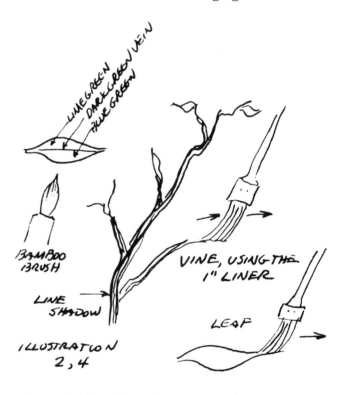

Stone Walls (Illus. 5, next page)

Lightly draw in the pattern of the stones with chalk. Use the 2" liner dipped in bluish gray paint to stroke in the *shadow* facets on the surface of the rocks. Choose one or two facets on each stone and lightly stroke in the highlights with light gray paint on natural burlap or white paint on eggshell burlap. Use the 1" liner with dark blue gray to suggest the cracks between stones, but *do not outline* every stone.

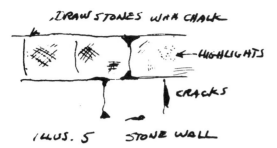

ILLUS. 5   STONE WALL

Wood Graining (Illus. 6)

Study pieces of wood to learn grain patterns. Notice how the grain grows thick and thin. Chalk in the width of the boards. Hold the 1" lining brush perpendicular to the painting surface.

ILLUS. 6   WOOD GRAINING

Lead with the narrow edge for thin strokes. Where the grains of wood approach and go around a knot, they become wider. Increase the pressure to increase the width of line. Against a medium brown tone, or natural burlap, use a light beige brown for the grain. With a lighter burlap, such as eggshell, use a darker brown. Shadow with bluish brown or highlight with pale yellow. Wood graining is improved by using the stubby little brush to add a bit of shadow and color.

Decor Without Painting

Do not overlook the use of variously patterned cloths as covering fabrics, especially denim, which comes in all sorts of designs and is structurally rugged enough for the flap hinging. Striped denims make wonderful "hallway backing" screens. Indian Head is also strong and comes in fine solid shades. Often burlap hinging can be used as "accent" over other fabrics. In this case, the vertical raw edges of the hinge must be folded under. For an extremely neat appearance, the burlap can be blind-stapled on one side as in upholstery. With wallpaper, cloth hinging must be on top. Also remember that wallpaper usually comes 18 inches wide, and battens must underlie all joints, if it is to be joined by stapling.

Detailing by Paint
Stencil & Spray

Here is a system of applying detail which yields surprisingly good results without requiring the skills of brushwork. The system is one of creating an image by multiple stencil patterns. For the example, the

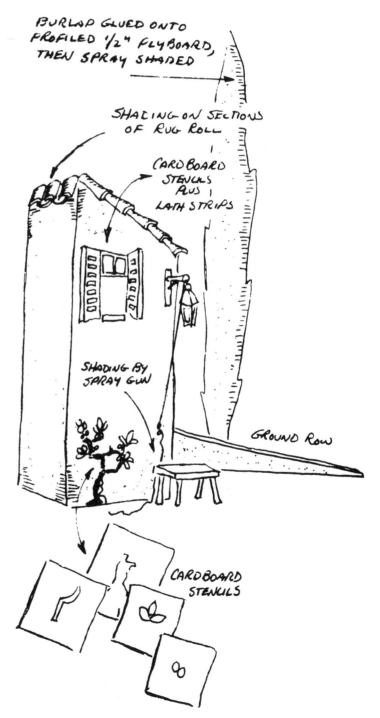

berry bush growing against the rustic building is made up of four separate stencils: trunk, branch, leaves and berries. By studying the bush it will be seen that the skillful maneuvering of the branch stencil provides the entire branch structure. This is also true of the leaves and berries. The one drawback to this system is the time consumed in changing the paint in the spray gun can. With a little planning, however, this can be minimized. Complete all scenery, then do all pieces involving one color, regardless of whether it be stencil or just shading. For example, the tree may be shaded with the same color as that for the leaves of the berry bush.

One of the advantages of stencil and spray is the crispness of the imagery; however, if a soft-edged effect is desired, hold the stencil slightly away from the surface of the fabric. Crispness of image is especially desirable in sign making. For many, it is much easier to sketch out the letters on cardboard or heavy Kraft paper and prepare a stencil with the utility knife than it is to letter directly onto the finished surface with brush, particularly if it is a textured one, such as burlap. For lettering by stencil and spray, the stencil should be stapled temporarily to the surface in many places. This would include the centers of O's, A's, R's and such.

Further Texturing

There are certain covering materials such as Upson Board and Masonite which are sheer, or nearly so, in texture . . . as in towers, serpentine walls, etc. These surfaces should be textured before paint is applied. In addition to mixing sawdust in the paint, there are various kinds of prepared papier machés on the market. Of particular usefulness is Theatremold, sold in 50-pound sacks by the Alcone Co., 32 West 20th St., New York, NY 10011.

When texturing surfaces which will be broken into segments for handling, such as a tower, run a knife down the joints just before the papier maché has completely dried. Such textured surfaces can be painted by spray or brush, or both, one after the other.

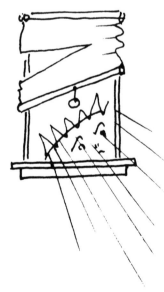

DRAMATIC LIGHTING

Good lighting can make bad scenery look OK and good scenery look even better. But what about the teacher whose classroom has broken window shades? Obviously, any scenery that is to be truly useful must be able to pass muster in broad daylight, and the scenery described in this book will be able to do just that! So, in order that proper stage lighting not appear a necessity, the subject of stage lighting was omitted from earlier editions of this book.

This may have been unwise. It is included now.

The Broken Window Shade

We watch the late afternoon sun streaking in below a large cloud mass after a spring shower. We see the delicate shadows of bare trees upon a leaf-strewn lawn of Indian summer, of the thin gold dusk of a winter afternoon. And we exclaim, "The lighting is so dramatic!" And rightly, for dramatic illumination awakens our sensibilities. It "puts things in a fresh light," to use a figurative phrase quite literally.

There is a great deal of mystique surrounding stage lighting, including numerous slang terms for specialized equipment, the "sacredness" of cue sheets, etc., but "lighting" really amounts to little more than getting some illumination onto a particular scene from the best possible angles and then being able to control the intensities of the light sources. One reason that the lighting for Broadway shows is constantly acclaimed is that designers assemble rental equipment from scratch for each production, whereas the dullness of lighting in more "institutional" theatres can be attributed to the fact that spotlights are purchased along with the building; thus, they tend to remain where they are first installed and are infrequently relocated or readjusted thereafter.

For small theatricals, a considerable amount of spotlighting equipment can be fashioned from the wide variety of PAR lamps by adding mounting gimbals, hoods and color holders. In the long run, however, I believe one is better served by purchasing standard spotlights. There are two principal types in use today — the Fresnel and the ellipsoidal. The Fresnel produces a variable, soft-edged field of light, with considerable flare, so that it is often necessary to use short tubes called snoots or high hats to avoid unwanted spillage. The ellipsoidal produces a fixed-spread, basically hard-edged field of illumination. The beam shape may be altered and the size reduced through the use of shutters, iris or templates, and

patterns may be introduced. And, where necessary, the normally hard-edged field can be softened in varying degrees through the use of many new diffusion filters, especially the Rosco OTF-2 Opal Tough Frost.

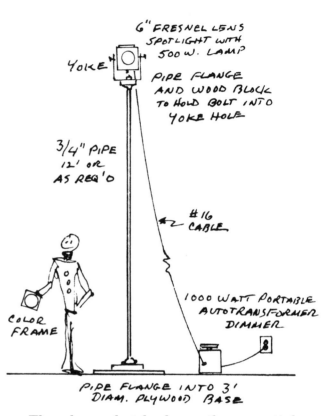

The above sketch shows the essential parts of dramatic illumination: a luminaire and its mounting device, a cable connection to a dimmer, the dimmer itself and its connection to a power source, in this instance, a nearby convenience outlet, usually good for 15 amperes and often 20. All these parts could probably be assembled for around $135. The only difference between the above and a complex Broadway show is a matter of enlargement and sophistication. I have known theatrical troupes to tour the country with 18 stands, a variety of spotlights, and a dozen dimmers. If a large-capacity electrical connection can be made, the dimmers are plugged into a multiple circuit box. If such a connection is impractical, then long extension cords are taken to as many separately fused convenience outlets as may be required.

The First Lighting Demonstration

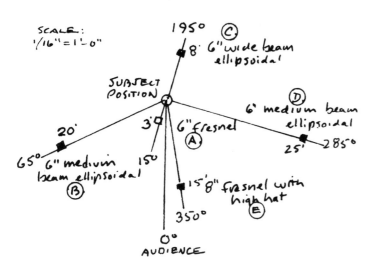

the spotlights. Record the spotlights in order of brightness, starting with the brightest as determined from the dimmer readings. In all probability an average will be C-D-B-A-E or C-B-D-A-E. This exercise will give the students a far better sense of what directional illumination and intensity control will do than any amount of formal instruction. And the most important lesson to be learned is that while you always need some light, from the front you don't need very much; in fact, a lot of it makes the scene go dead.

Arrange the equipment above as diagrammed on a spotlight mounting grid about 15' above the stage floor, with all spotlights aimed at the Subject Position, where actors or scenery will be placed. Each spotlight must be controlled by a separate dimmer, and the dimmers should be located at the Audience Position. Let each student in turn dim each spotlight up and down in rotation to get the feel of them, then let each student light the scene to his own satisfaction by arranging the dimmer levels of all

The Second Lighting Demonstration

(A) is a 6" wide-beam ellipsoidal spotlight on a low stand behind the masking screen. Its field of illumination is restricted to the archway by means of framing shutters. This will cause a long shadow of Hamlet to precede his entrance. (B) is a gooseneck or music stand light to make a window cloth glow. (C) is a 6" narrow-beam ellipsoidal spotlight with pattern template

suggesting light that has passed through a stained glass window some distance away. (D) is an 8" Fresnel spotlight with lavender or blue color filter and snoot, kept as dim as possible consistent with visibility, for it plays no part in the light motivation for the scene.

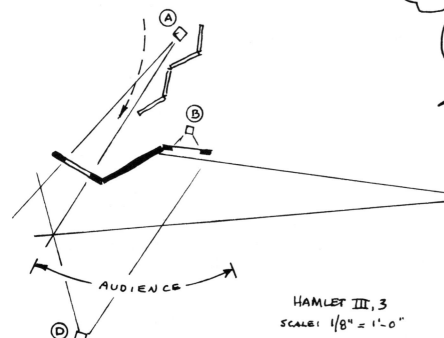

HAMLET III, 3
SCALE: 1/8" = 1'-0"

The Third Lighting Demonstration

Scene: interior, simple dwelling, by night, with candlelight

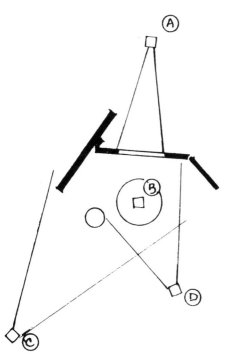

Backlight (A) is a 6" wide-beam ellipsoidal spotlight framed to the archway, with blue-green color filter, to light cloth stretched across rear of shuttered doors for "chink" effect, or to provide path of moonlight through archway when shutters are open. (B) is a hooded 6" Fresnel downlight directly over the table, with amber filter. (C) is an 8" Fresnel spotlight, hooded, with steel blue filter, for visibility purposes under night conditions. (D) is a 6" Fresnel spotlight, hooded, with amber filter, for touching up the central area of the scene with candle glow, in effect, bringing some of the candle glow around where the audience can see it on the actors.

Consistent throughout these examples is the use of soft-edged spotlights for strictly frontal, or "fill," lighting. Ellipsoidal spotlights in forward positions should be used only where a spotlighting "effect" is desired and with iris control instead of the usual framing shutters in order to avoid angular cut-off lines.

These examples suggest that lighting for the open stage is quite different than lighting for the proscenium stage. Since there is no proscenium "frame," there is no need to use frontal ellipsoidal spotlights in order to mask light off the "frame." Nor is there a contained stage space, hence border lights are inapplicable. The frontal "fill" Fresnel spotlights take over the job that the border lights do in a contained stage space. Special Fresnel lenses are available which spread the light sideways for this purpose. Such lenses are called "oval beam" lenses.

Those familiar with the McCandless system of cross lighting the actor — the "45°-45°" frontal system — will notice its absence in the three lighting demonstrations. This system develped out of proscenium staging, and I do not believe it is applicable under space stage conditions, especially with the greater freedom in selecting spotlight mounting positions. Besides, it is a very expensive way to light a show.

One of the most important factors in lighting for set-piece staging is the nature of the overall background such as dark velour or an evenly lit cyclorama. The three lighting demonstrations ignore this factor because most space stagers aren't in a position to control the background. The reader is directed to the Architectural Section for information on backgrounds.

The above lighting examples presume that the place of performance can be darkened. This is not always so. Those with limited budgets might well consider the technique of "overlighting," that is, using whatever general illumination there is, but touching up the dramatic action and the scenery with a powerful spotlight or two.

Tips for Good Lighting

1. The fewer the sources of illumination, the more dramatic the scene will appear.

2. Control equipment is equally as important as lighting equipment.

3. Shadows are softened by the use of roughly textured scenic materials.

4. Light falling on dyed or rough material appears more pleasant and realistic than light on smooth, painted surfaces.

5. By keeping frontal spotlights to a minimum, the multiple shadows of actors are reduced.

6. Frontal lighting beams should be soft-edged, to avoid sharp cut-off lines.

7. Scenery which possesses radiance in itself through the use of translucent screens, windows, lanterns and concealed floodlighting, reduces the amount of light required for the dramatic action.

Selection of Equipment

6" and 8" Fresnel lens spotlights with 500 and 1000 watt lamps are standard market items. Selecting ellipsoidal spotlights is a bit more complicated, since there are different beam spreads and options for shaping the beam. In the 6" diameter lens category I use the medium-spread spotlight with dual 6" x 9" plano-convex lenses and with four framing shutters, and also the narrow-spread with 6" x 12" lenses, but in place of the framing shutters I use iris shutters or template slots in about equal numbers. Some 4½" wide-spread spotlights are useful also. All these spotlights can use 500-watt lamps.

These wattages should provide from 30 to 50 foot candles at the subject position with a mounting height around 14 or 15 feet, and depending on how the spotlights are colored and dimmed for the "balancing" of a scene.

The desire for simpler methods of controlling a large number of variably dimmed circuits and for a lightweight dimmer as well has led to the development of highly sophisticated electronic systems which are not, however, without their problems — problems which were not inherent in the older resistance and autotransformer dimming systems. The problems have to do with dimmer hum, lamp filament hum, and both radiated and conducted eletromagnetic interference to sound systems, etc. Manufacturers can reduce these problems to acceptable levels through proper filters and chokes, but these cost money. Generally, the more expensive the dimmer the better its performance will be. But unless the buyer can test the proposed dimmer unit with an oscilloscope, he had best "road test" one by loading up all the dimmer channels to full capacity and setting the dimmers to a half reading, for it is at this position that humming and interference will be at maximum. It is also a good idea to plug in a radio nearby.

As to lamps, while "quartz" burns cleaner and has a longer life than "incandescents," the lamps are expensive, rather delicate, and burn hotter, thus requiring stronger and more costly color filters.

Color Filters

In my own work I use color sparingly and only where there is a strong motivation for it. With the exception of the more delicate tints, color diminishes the intensity of the illumination considerably, not to mention its effect on scenery and costumes. Color is a vast subject and a matter of individual artistic preference. The best way to proceed here is to send for the Olesen Co. catalog (1535 Ivar Ave., Hollywood, CA 90028) and study the various sections on color filters and diffusion media. Rosco also has excellent technical literature for the asking (Rosco Laboratories, Inc., 36 Bush Ave., Port Chester, NY 10573).

SCENIC PROGRESSION

By scenic progression is meant the manner by which scenery is arranged for the flow of the dramatic action. Those familiar only with the proscenium stage may never have given the subject much thought, other than to recall the mad scramble to change settings when the curtain closed on a scene. But this sort of "scene" change refers entirely to the proscenium stage and "changeable scenery," that is, one set replacing another in the same stage space, which is the way things are when a set forms a complete "picture" and ties into the frame.

When you don't have a frame, such scenery is, of course, redesigned and becomes an object in space. And with the absence of the frame also comes the lack of any external guide to the size of the scenery, so the scenic object in space can be any size the designer wants it to be.

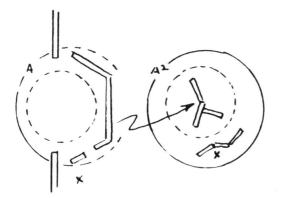

This transition from a framed space to an open space is shown in the pair of diagrams above. The perimeter or "box set" turns into a freestanding set piece, and instead of surrounding the acting area, it now sits within it. And while "backstage" has gone with the proscenium, any necessary "off-stage" space (x) can be created temporarily by a masking screen.

Not only is the scenery exactly the size the designer wants it, but consider the size of the playing area itself. Does circle (A^2)

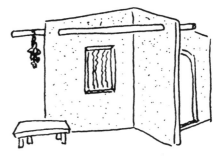

have to be the same size as (A), for the conditions which set size (A) have been eliminated?

As the expression goes, "It's a whole new ball game." If the size of the playing area and the size of the scenery are both optional, the playing area, in consequence, is just a large game board, and the actors and scenery, tokens upon it. And while the dramatic action is naturally sequential, it is no longer necessary to have the scenery sequentially displayed or to use scenery so designed that separate settings are mutually exclusive of one another.

Another way of looking at it is by pretending a stage is an ice cream store, with the scenes of a play as boxes of vanilla, strawberry, chocolate, etc., also some boxes of the Neapolitan and marbled varieties. The picture frame stage sells the pure flavors, one box or one scene at a time. The space stage sells the combinations: flavors or scenes are distinguishable, but are stacked simultaneously (the Neapolitan) or more subtly interspliced (the marbled).

As a result, the director and the scene designer must work very closely together in the interweaving of the dramatic action and the settings so that the play may flow smoothly over the stage from scene to scene with a minimum of interruption from things technical. In order to distribute scenes properly over the performance space, I find it essential to chart the action of the play in terms of both the playing times and number of actors in scenes. Scenes with the greater number of people and the longer playing times should be programmed for the central parts of the playing area, while shorter and less populous scenes can be staged to the sides. Attempt no more scenery than is absolutely necessary. Small set pieces can be moved quickly during illumination changes or musical segues. Note particularly the concept of "shared" space, that is, neutral areas between set pieces being included in the lighting for a nearby scene. Cf. page 37 (b)(c).

One should not hesitate to make full use of the "game board" concept of a playing area despite fear of audience disapproval. In the first place, one must realize that in the recorded traditions of theatre, proscenium staging is the novelty amidst dozens of ways of expressing dramatic environments. In the second place, that there is no better way to accomplish these ends under the given circumstances will be self-evident, and if they are accomplished well, this is what makes style, and audiences are quick to recognize and applaud it.

THE ARCHITECTURAL SECTION

Found Spaces

One of the reasons for the popularity of self-supporting scenery is its deployment just about anywhere there is a flat floor. And dramatic illumination can be added if there is at least 12' of height. Entrances and exits are reworked with folding screen sets, and these same screens provide offstage space as well. Of course, subdued architectural decor such as is found in art galleries makes the most satisfactory background. And a rug does wonders for a playing area. It "sets the stage," so to speak, for something special to happen. And scenery always looks better upon it. Furthermore, a note of intimacy is added when the playing area is distinguished from the remainder of the flat floor in a room, especially in gyms. Carpet is clean to work on, since the dirt sifts down through the pile to await the vacuum cleaner, whereas dirt on a floor contaminates everything that touches it. While most acting areas are rectangular, and about 18' x 24', a square rug will be the more practical shape when two-sided seating is involved. I recommend the purchase of four 12x12's. Select an autumn color in plush pile and do *not* use a cushion.

A flat-floor situation can be improved by the use of "band risers," and these are obtainable in heights of 8", 16" and 24". Write the Wenger Corp., 576 Park Drive, Owatonna, MN 55060 for a catalog, and study the various arrangements of such risers.

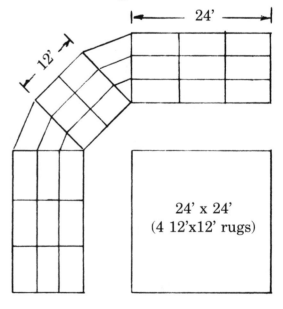

24' x 24'
(4 12'x12' rugs)

Arrangement of Band-Orchestra Risers
Scale: 1/16" = 1'-0"

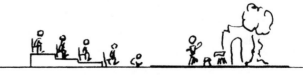

The reason that seating should not flank more than two sides of the playing area in flat-floor situations is to prevent the scenery from being forced to the rear, which is contrary to the natural placement of such scenery. Where risers are unobtainable, no more than two rows of chairs are practical. A considerable number of children can be on mats down front.

A stage platform is not a good solution for two reasons: movement to the stage is made more difficult by the change in level, and, for sightlines, the audience should sit on one side only.

Acoustics in Found Spaces

In "found" spaces the acoustics of the room may prove to be the most difficult problem of all. When it is hard to understand the human voice, any one or a combination of the following three conditions may be the cause:

(1) too large a volume of space for the size of the sound source,

(2) too long a reverberation time before the sound decays, or,

(3) too long a time delay between sound heard directly and the same sound returning from the reflecting surfaces.

Electronic amplification is the only remedy for overly large spaces and to deal with an actor in motion requires both sophisticated equipment and highly trained operators. There is something that the amateur can do about the remaining conditions, however, and this is to "dampen" the sound at strategic places by the introduction of what is known in the "trade" as acoustical "fuzz," fiberglass board or blankets from 2" to 4" thick, or two layers of heavy flannel (or cotton velour) hung at least 6" from a wall.

In order to determine where to place such absorptive material, some knowledge about how sound works is necessary. Condi-

tion (3) can be illustrated by a simple diagram, and remedial action here may also correct Condition (2), though this is not always the case. A very wide room is used as an illustration because this shape can be very troublesome.

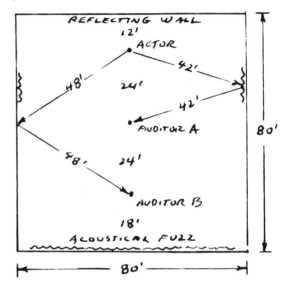

Speech intelligibility is threatened when the *difference* in linear feet between the path of sound going to and returning from a reflecting surface and the path of sound coming directly to an auditor is as little as 50'.

For Auditor A, the path of the direct sound is 24', while the indirect is 84', or a difference of 60'. "Fuzzing" the side wall at this point will be helpful.

On the other hand, for Auditor B the path of reflected sound is 96' while the direct sound travels 48', or a difference of 48'. Leaving the wall surface reflective helps.

The wall to the rear of the audience should be fuzzed so that Auditor A does not hear the direct sound at 24' plus the reflected sound from the rear wall at 108', a difference of 84'.

The foregoing is based on a plan study only. To be accurate, a section of the room should also be studied, since a properly located ceiling plane might so assist hearing for Auditor A that the effect of the reflection from the side wall would be minimized.

Using an Existing Stage

In all likelihood, the stage will be a raised one and proscenium in style. The proscenium aspect is the one more easily solved, by observing the principle of keeping the set pieces out in space and away from the frame. If there is a choice between a curtain cyclorama and a sky cyclorama, choose the curtains, otherwise all entrances will have to be from the sides. If the curtains are velour and dark in color, it will be easier to light the stage than if the curtains are beige, or worse yet, of that light gray vinyl fabric so popular with school administrators for its indestructibility. Again, folding screen sets will be of great assistance in working out many entrances and exits.

A raised stage of 3' or more is contrary to the aesthetics of space staging. Actors and scenery look best when they are in truly three-dimensional relationships. Thus, the higher the stage the less of this effect there is. And a raised stage becomes a real problem when the eye level of spectators falls below the level of the stage. The only remedy for this is to bring the action as far forward as possible.

Planning a Theatre with Self-Supporting Scenery in Mind

There are not too many instances of just building a theatre *for* self-supporting scenery. When it comes to spending that much money, the "theatre of literal illusion" is usually thrown in for good measure, despite the costs for a proscenium frame with working loft, additional off-stage space, and more stringent fire codes.

However, if it is a "shared space" that you are talking about, one that can be used for assembly, concert, forum, etc., then it can be said generally that any space which is suitable for the sort of self-supporting scenery this book is all about will also be suitable for the above-mentioned activities. Definitely the proscenium form will not, though all too often it must by necessity be used for all these activities.

Diagram (A) below shows the traditional "concert" plan, the "shoe-box" shape, where the audience sits directly before an orchestra, so that the sound is in proper perspective. For the same reason, the view onto the low platform is excellent for drama, for there is a visual perspective common to all. And if the audience is terraced, so much the better, for the dimensional relationships of the set pieces are improved. Speech

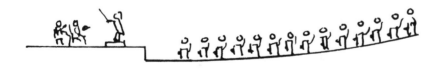

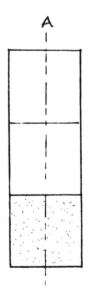

Two classic solutions for seating in the concert hall "A" plan configuration: the maximum "dished" slope, and terraces with 1' risers, each with a 2' platform.

acoustics are obtained by the deployment of flannel curtains which change the reverberation time. For a shared program a concert theatre may very well be the best choice of all.

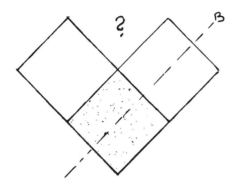

Diagram (B) above shows a classic seating plan with the audience on two adjacent sides of a playing area. One immediately thinks of the ancient theatre at Knossus in Crete and of the Japanese NoH theatre. This is similar to the Wenger band riser solution given earlier. It is, in effect, half of a "theatre in the round" where the playing area is square or rectangular. The "?" area is one difficult to design for seating. It can be chamfered, as in the preceding band riser diagram. In arena staging, with a rectangular playing space, entrances are located at the corners for this reason. The seating terraces for this arrangement should have 12" or 14" risers, with the playing area at ground level.

Diagram (C), right, shows about the same playing area reshaped for a theatre for a quarter-circle seating. The seating is much improved and of greater capacity, al-

though the playing area is not as intimate. The dashed line indicates the one bad actor-audience relationship. The playing area can be on a slightly elevated platform, and the seating can be of maximum slope, or terraces,

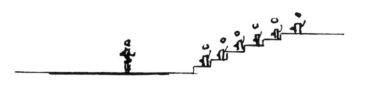

Typical seating for "B" plan with ground level playing area and 3' terraces with 1'-2" risers. Seating at ground level not recommended because of cross-lighting.

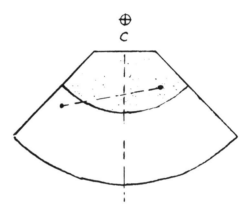

or both. An example of a quarter-circle seating theatre with open stage is given on the following page. This sort of design can be inserted into a very economical building shape.

Excluded from our studies are the thrust and arena theatres where the audience sits on three or all four sides of the playing area. The sort of unitary scenery this book is all about does not work well on these stages.

Typical seating for "C" plan with low 1'-6" platform, 1:10 slope, cross-aisle, and 1:3 terraces.

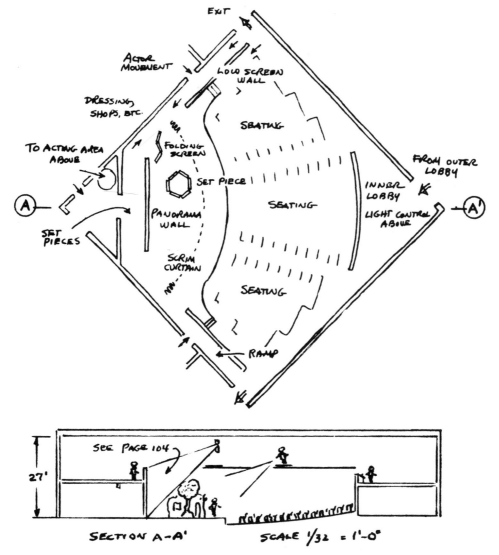

EXIT

ACTOR MOVEMENT

LOW SCREEN WALL

DRESSING SHOPS, ETC.

SEATING

TO ACTING AREA ABOVE

FOLDING SCREEN

SET PIECE

SEATING

FROM OUTER LOBBY

INNER LOBBY

A

SET PIECES

PANORAMA WALL

SEATING

LIGHT CONTROL ABOVE

A'

SCRIM CURTAIN

SEATING

RAMP

SEE PAGE 104

27'

SECTION A-A'   SCALE 1/32 = 1'-0"

With the thrust stage, any scenery but the most skeletal must be moved to the rear and should be redesigned as "facade" scenery. And since this type of scenery is considerably larger, its handling is simplified by the addition of a shallow proscenium stagehouse with rigging and wings. This can be a very expensive solution, however, and the flexibility is lost that comes with the use of unitary scenery as focal points of action on a frank space stage. As for arena, scenery here is custom-made and inserted as profiles between the spectators and the playing area both above and below sightlines.

To change a concert hall (diagram A) into a working proscenium theatre, one would only have to add the stage mask or "picture frame" plus the stagehouse with its wing spaces and rigging loft. However, with unitary, self-supporting scenery there is no need for stage rigging, nor do wing spaces have to be as large. So those who like the proscenium frame for ease of stage movement and obvious subtleties in lighting positions can build a "modified" proscenium theatre quite inexpensively, yet do some very effective staging. A word of warning is in order, however. When a "modified" proscenium theatre is built, the owner must be very sure that unitary scenery, and only unitary scenery, will be used on the stage and that transient designers don't attempt the sort of scenery which requires a working loft stagehouse and expanded wing space.

Inspiration for the modified proscenium theatre comes from "store window" display.

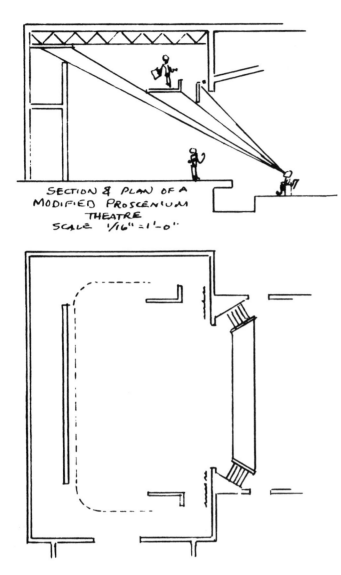

SECTION & PLAN OF A
MODIFIED PROSCENIUM
THEATRE
SCALE 1/16" = 1'-0"

Colored Shadow Projection

With set-piece staging, the space above the playing area is free for illumination, and, under certain conditions, the illumination may include a system for adding backgrounds by projection, thus extending the environment suggested by a set piece, such as adding a city skyline beyond an apartment unit or a grove of cottonwood trees behind the adobe house in the sketch below. Although the system is shown here in a modified proscenium theatre, it can be worked into any theatre space that can provide the projection catwalk and the horizontal masking as shown on page 100.

In selecting a particular system of background projection, several considerations were kept in mind: economy, of course, both in terms of installation and operation, and in terms of time as well as of materials and equipment, together with an awareness of the marked tendency towards the abstract in the design of space stage scenery.

It is textbook orthodoxy with display men that any scenery in store windows takes the form of "set pieces" in a neutral, architectural environment, such as duvetyn-covered panels, etc. In fact, the beauty and compactness of first-class store window display has influenced many stage designers.

Wall covered with textured vinyl — light gray blue.

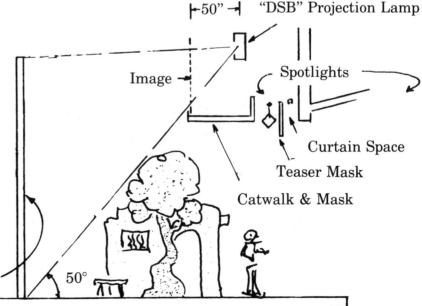

Lamphouse with "DSB" Projection Lamp

|←50"→|

Image

Spotlights

Curtain Space

Teaser Mask

Catwalk & Mask

50°

Sectional drawing at scale of ⅛" = 1'-0"

The end result of the system is the projection of a shadowgraph over actors and set pieces onto some form of background wall. The technical means by which this is accomplished is by combining the smallest possible lamp filament consistent with the necessary brilliance *and* the maximum practical distance between the lamp filament and the image for the largest image possible consistent with sightlines. Any resemblance to Linnebach technique is superficial, for while the principle remains the same, a "shadow" device, the conditions are considerably altered, and the results quite different.

The Technical Parts

It was Thomas Wilfred who first rearranged the traditional Linnebach elements by separating the lamp housing and the image plane, and since he had a different artistic result in mind, he renamed his shadow projection system *The Direct Beam*. Wilfred was seeking a reasonable amount of clarity as well as the highly suggestive and hazy Linnebach patterns. By distancing the image from the lamp filament, he

of materials from which images could be fashioned. And the problem of distortion was gotten rid of for all time since it is an easy matter to keep the image parallel to a projection surface when it is no longer a part of the lamphouse.

Wilfred worked mainly with imagery painted with transparent dyes upon clear acetate sheets. Since these sheets came in 40" widths, his maximum image height was limited to 40". And his favorite projection lamp was the 60-volt, 2100-watt T24/8, with a biplane filament approximately ⅝" square.

In order to achieve "time-of-day" flexibility with his imagery, he contrived an ingenious color-changing device which consisted of matched frames containing glass strips in a variety of widths and stained as desired by transparent dyes. The frames were then suspended across the light aperture in the lamphouse on a common cord which ran over a pulley. By turning the pulley very slowly, the color strips, some ascending, others descending, and too close to the light source for any sense of "focus"

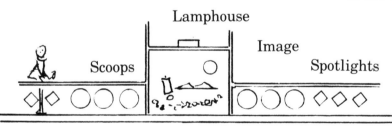

Elevation of Projection Catwalk

This drawing is further explained on page 104, column 2.

accomplished the clarity, and by intercepting the path of light between the lamphouse and the image, he could recover the haziness when he desired.

The separation of the image from the lamphouse brought two additional results of great importance. Any effect of radiant heat from the lamp upon the image was eliminated, thereby increasing the variety

whatever, altered the color of the light passing through to the image, and dawn and dusk transitions, etc., were accomplished. And by connecting the pulley to a 1 RPM motor on dimmer, the control was placed in the hands of the light man.

In my own work in small theatre design, in the majority of instances, I have the advantage of not requiring a projection lamp brilliance over 1000 watts, thereby gaining additional clarity because of a smaller filament, and, instead of the "color changer" as a transitional device, I conceived of imagery in terms of multiple light sources, by adding a number of 500-watt "scoops" to each side of the "image," thereby altering the method by which transitions are accomplished and reducing dependence on clear acetate sheets for imagery.

The practical maximum to which the "separation of imagery from the projection lamp filament" can be pushed is reflected in the ⅛" sectional drawing on page 101. To increase this distance would be impractical because either the masking would have to be too low, compromising the acting space, or the lamphouse too high, thus "raising the roof" both physically and cost-wise, for the lamphouse is just grazing the trusses now. Thus, it is the arrangement of parts which dictates the degree of clarity, and it is up to the designer to recognize this and to prepare his imagery accordingly.

From experience, it is possible to provide two rules of thumb. On the one hand, it is usually possible to obtain a lamp-to-image separation that is 100 x the filament width. On the other hand, given the above, the designer will achieve an illusion of clarity if he restricts any line work in his imagery to not less than ¼".

The ⅛" section shows the DSB lamp for maximum brilliance, but since the catwalk is only 15' above the stage floor, the DDB and CZX lamps can be used as well, with a marked increase in image clarity if the 50" distance is maintained. If it is the practice to inter-change lamps, then the DRS instead of the DSB would simplify things. Both filaments are the same, though the DSB is the more durable lamp.

On the other hand, when an image has been painted with transparent dyes on a standard acetate sheet of 40" width, which is then the maximum image height, a smaller filament would enable the lamphouse to be moved closer without a loss in detail.

The maximum image size, which in turn sets the catwalk framework, is unknown until both the dimensions and location of the background wall are set and the location of the lamphouse established. The diagram below shows how this is done.

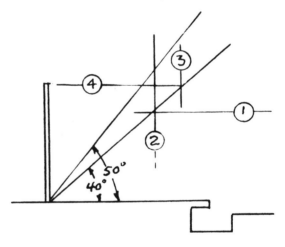

In the diagram, known factors are the location and height of the background wall, also the limits of the lower angle of projection. Possibly given is (1) or the ceiling line.

Catwalk Height	Lamp	Lamp Base	Watts	Image-to-Lamp Distance
15'	CZX	Med. Pf.	500	31"
16-17'	DDB	Med. Pf.	750	40"
18'	DRS	Med. Pf.	1000	50"
18'	DSB	Mog. Pf.	1000	50"

The intersection of line (1) with whatever projection lower limit angle is desired establishes the theoretical "bottom of image" point along line (2). Select the appropriate lamp from the lamp chart, which will establish line (3). The intersection of line (3) with the desired lower limit projection angle line will establish the filament point. Line (4) connects the filament with the top of the background wall, thus establishing the theoretical height of the image. The study is finalized when ceiling mask and catwalk structuring is completed. In this diagram, no allowance was made for the thickness of the ceiling plane under the catwalk and the structure of the catwalk itself.

It is fairly obvious that plans for a theatre which include the overhead background projection system must be drawn up very carefully, and inspection during construction is continually necessary because any worker can inadvertently foul up the lighting freeway with pipes, ducts, conduits, not to mention getting the structural parts such as the catwalk, etc., in the wrong place.

The lamphouse may be made of almost any kind of metal box. The interior must be flat black. In a pinch, a 6" stovepipe and elbow will serve, though an 8" stovepipe is better. The elbow serves as a light trap at the top of the pipe. The size of the light aperture can be plotted from the sectional and plan drawings of the theatre.

The drawing, scaled at 1" = 1'-0", shows an 8" stovepipe and elbow about the lamp assembly of CZX lamp, medium prefocus base, and yoke of perforated pipe strap. The strap should be secured to the stovepipe in such a way that the axis coincides with the filament position. This is to enable the lamp to be tipped forward about 10° both to improve brilliance and to avoid "ghost" images due to reflectance from the glass envelope.

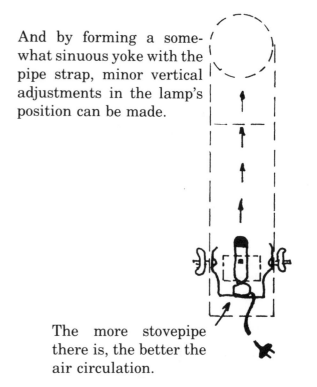

And by forming a somewhat sinuous yoke with the pipe strap, minor vertical adjustments in the lamp's position can be made.

The more stovepipe there is, the better the air circulation.

The scoops must be of the type which have diffuse alzak aluminum reflectors and which use the mogul screw inside frost PS incandescent lamps of 300 or 500 watts. Tungsten-halogen (quartz) lamps, because of their miniature size and regardless of inside frosting or not, tend to cause "hot spots" on the background wall when partially dimmed. The "rule of thumb" on quantity is one scoop per color circuit per 10' of background wall. The background wall shown is 30' wide, so ideally there should be nine scoops for a full three-color circuit service. Six are shown in the drawing on page 102.

Image Construction

One of the most effective images can be made by lashing a real tree limb with branches and leaves across the image area, which, in this case, is 5' x 7'. Suspend an amber or orange color filter a few inches away from the lamphouse aperture. Place chocolate-color filters in a set of scoops. Effect: woods scene at dusk. With purple or urban blue in another set of scoops, a very nice transition may be made into night. Start dimming the projection lamp first, then gradually segue from the chocolate to the deep blue. Moving from a projection to a pure color permits the image to be replaced, since duplicate projection systems are impractical when the amount of space taken up by one is considered.

In order of increasing complexity, the next image should be made up of cuts in a 5' x 7' opaque area, such as heavy Kraft paper. This is the sort of image shown in the projection catwalk elevation drawing on page 102. In contrast to the above image, here the scoops establish the overall field of color and the detail is superimposed upon this field in terms of patterns of light, light-upon-light, so to speak. Blue-green color filters for a set of scoops is appropriate for this image. Colors should also be taped over the cuts in the Kraft paper, with the exception of the boat sail, which will be white. I suggest a yellow moon, a different blue for the island, a yellow-green for the shoreline greenery, and the boat hull, an orange. And while there will be no line of demarcation between sea and sky, the flat island bottom will suggest one. The projection lamp should be at full; the scoops dimmed somewhat. The image-maker may be quite surprised at the lack of color blend with scoops and projection lamp combined, and this can be explained by three factors: (1) the projected light is brighter, (2) the projected light is in terms of precise patterns, and (3) the mind has the uncanny ability to reassign color values to suggestive forms which relate to things known to memory.

The next image (below left), a city skyline at night, is a combination of the two preceding image techniques. The projection filament provides the night sky and moon disc and also the lighted windows, with yellow taped over the apertures in the cardboard, while the scoops fill in the building area. Chocolate is suggested for the scoops. If more sky is desired, merely move the image down in the frame and cut off the unwanted portion at the bottom. The sky area can be textured by a fold or two of nylon net stretched across and tacked down.

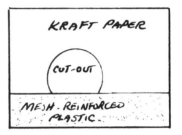

Continuing with the idea of "texturing," purchase some mesh-reinforced plastic such as "glass-o-net" and stretch it across the bottom of the image area as shown. With scoops deep blue and the lamphouse gate covered with lemon-yellow, one would get an effect of the desert at night, with the moon rising. The mesh-reinforced plastic has a lensatic action on the light passing through it, and dots of yellow light will be produced on the background wall.

Following the idea of "texture" a little further, purchase a piece of ⅛" hardware cloth. It may be necessary to relocate the lamphouse and go to a smaller filament if the hardware cloth cannot be obtained in

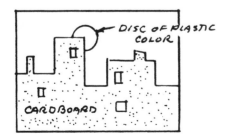

widths over 4'. With a heavy black Magic Marker on a sweep stick, score the outline of the moon, and, using duck-bill tin snips, *carefully* remove the moon disc. The silhouette of the earth berm and peony plant can be of cardboard wired to the mesh. With the projection lamp on, the basic effect is one of the moon floating in a "grayish" sky. Make no mistake in cutting out the disc, for each error will show up instantly. Dark green scoops are suggested. For an image of this sort, however, a "quality" sky is necessary. This is accomplished by stroking a pale green color filter about 8" x 10" with yellow Magic Marker or Colorine, keeping the strokes more or less parallel and with the strokes from ¼" to ½" apart. This color filter is then inserted into the path of light from the lamphouse at varying distances, from close up to about 6" away, until the sky takes on a vaguely textured quality.

At this point, one is ready to make a "Bali H'ai" island as seen from across the water from another island. Potted palms are brought to the catwalk deck and arranged at each side of the image area, to provide a "picture frame" for the view. Scoops will color these shadows dark green. The distant island is drawn with Colorine on a full sheet of pale blue color filter. Cut off areas around the island. Suspend the island by very fine wires between the lamphouse and the image. The very palest blue should be placed across the lamphouse aperture. The effect here is one of foreground, clear cut, "framing" the sea with the island in a distant haze, in very soft delineation.

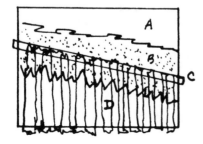

The composite image (below left) suggests a wheat field on a storm-threatened afternoon. (A) is open. The top edge of the Kraft paper (B) is cut to simulate the upper edge of scudding clouds, and a gray color filter covers (A). The lower edge of the Kraft paper is cut in a jagged vertical pattern to simulate the top profile of the wheat against dark clouds. A diagonal batten (C) passes across the Kraft paper to provide support for lemon yellow color filters (D) which are pleated and stapled down in irregular folds. Blue scoops at low intensity complete the scene. This image was originally created for a small projection area and was colored with gelatine sheets, which meant the image could be no wider than 24" for the gray. Some color filters now come in rolls 48" to 54" wide, enabling larger images to be fashioned in this manner.

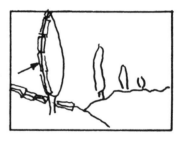

This image is made up of carefully fitted pieces of color filters with neatly taped joints of narrow strips of masking tape. Generally, a full-scale cartoon is drawn on Kraft paper or cardboard and the color filters cut out with a stencil knife. This technique is somewhat simplified if there can be an underlying transparent sheet the full size of the image. Tape strips should be about ⅛" wide. When ¼" or wider, a stained glass window effect begins to take over, although this may not be bad in all situations, since delineating the separation of color blocks adds "crispness" to an image.

A variation of the color mosaic technique was used for a view of the world from a space ship. An ellipsoidal spotlight with blue-green filter was focused on the background wall. Then the projection lamp was turned on and the diameter of the spotlight field measured at the image plane. A circle of similar diameter was scribed on a Kraft paper image and the continents plotted and removed. A straw or other appropriate color filter was placed across the lamphouse aperture, then the continents were superimposed onto the blue-green field of the spotlight, which represented ocean. The scoops were filtered deep blue. Thus a color mosaic was made with color filters without joints or without having to paint with dyes on a transparent sheet.

The images described above are but a random sampling of the possibilities of this art form. Not yet mentioned is imagery consisting of transparent dyes such as Magic Marker inks, lamp dips, dyes from stained-glass window kits, etc., brushed or swabbed onto clear acetate or lightly tinted transparent color filters. Rosco has a dye set. Clear acetate is normally available in 40" widths. For an economical base, Sears has a 48" super-clear vinyl. However, imagery created by this technique is usually the least satisfactory, possibly because it is very much like a "painting," whereas the scenery in front of it is dimensional and somewhat abstract. It also goes without saying that there is no way to get the dyes onto the transparent surface "anonymously," so to speak, and the artist's "style" in application must be considered part of the impression.

Rules of Thumb

(1) Avoid rendering in perspective nearby features such as fields, gardens, steps and terraces, and objects thereupon, such as "sheep in a pasture." Treat imagery in the manner of architectural elevations.

(2) With some imagery, such as a full silhouette, illumination from the projection lamp filament must extend across the complete background. But with the "light-on-light" technique, the scoops are responsible for the full color field and the image need not be the maximum size.

(3) Color filters for stage lighting are more vivid than lacquer dyes, lamp dips and felt pen inks.

(4) Heavily saturated color shades make better images and filters for floods than tints do. Also, the more saturated colors, even though of less intensity than tints, "hold up" better under interference from acting area illumination.

(5) Designs which involve blocks of color are more effective than intricate line work.

(6) A ¼" cut in a piece of Kraft paper projects more clearly than a ¼" opaque line drawn on a transparency.

(7) Regarding interference from acting area illumination, or "spill," the problem is not as serious as in the "theatre of literal illusion" because both the scenery and the projected imagery are more suggestive than facsimile. However, certain precautions must be taken:

(a) The stage floor must be non-reflective, that is, not varnished or waxed, and dark in tone. This is one advantage of carpet.

(b) Fresnel spotlights should be hooded.

(c) Any direct light falling upon the background wall should be from one light source only and soft-edged, that is, either from a Fresnel spotlight or from an ellipsoidal spotlight with a diffusion filter.

(d) If a projection rather than just plain color must be used for a brightly lit scene, bring the scene lights up slowly so that the projection may register before it fades.

On the Wings of a Folding Screen

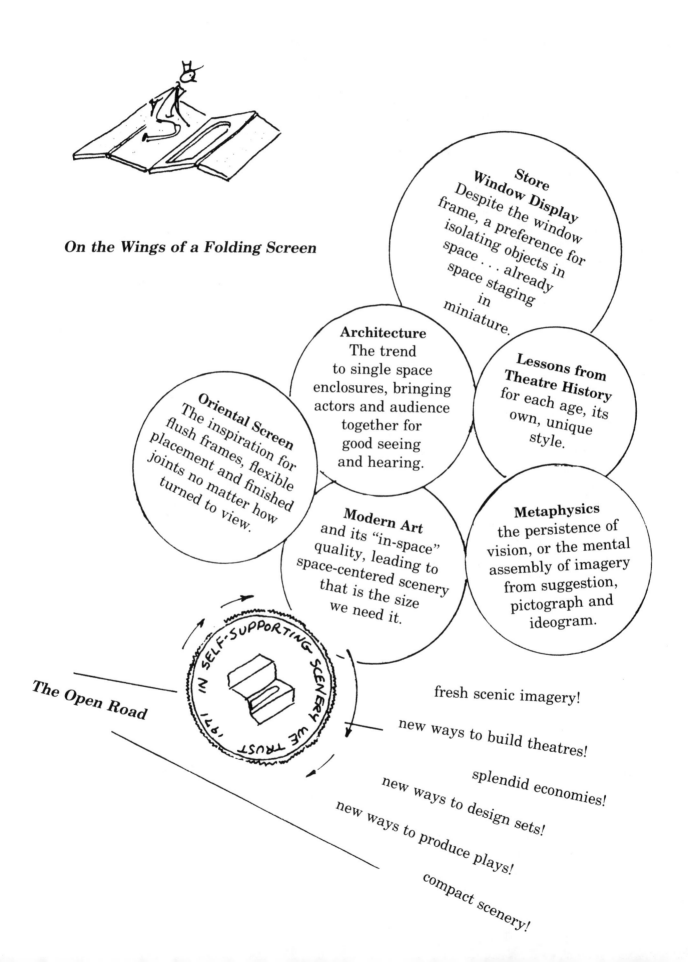

Store Window Display
Despite the window frame, a preference for isolating objects in space . . . already space staging in miniature.

Architecture
The trend to single space enclosures, bringing actors and audience together for good seeing and hearing.

Lessons from Theatre History
for each age, its own, unique style.

Oriental Screen
The inspiration for flush frames, flexible placement and finished joints no matter how turned to view.

Modern Art
and its "in-space" quality, leading to space-centered scenery that is the size we need it.

Metaphysics
the persistence of vision, or the mental assembly of imagery from suggestion, pictograph and ideogram.

IN SELF-SUPPORTING SCENERY WE TRUST 1971

The Open Road

fresh scenic imagery!

new ways to build theatres!

splendid economies!

new ways to design sets!

new ways to produce plays!

compact scenery!

SUPPLEMENT

Flat Framing
on Profile Board

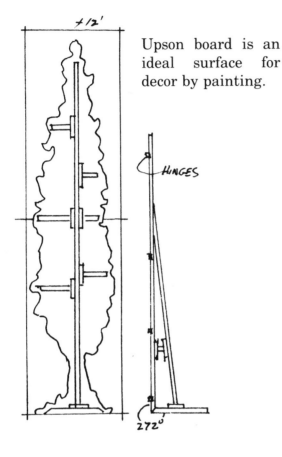

Upson board is an ideal surface for decor by painting.

Place ³⁄₁₆" sheets of Upson board face down on work table. Prepare flat framing members by fitting shoes and positioning. Trace outlines on sheets. Coat both these areas and also undersides of framing members with Elmer's glue. When in place, secure temporarily with partially driven nails which pass into table top. Let dry for several hours. Then carefully remove nails and secure shoes to stile and rail. Prepare brace jack and hinge to stile.

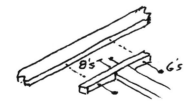

Flat Framing on Profile Board
Cloth Flap Hinged

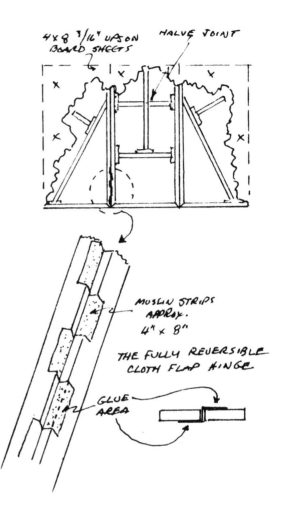

Lay the panels side by side face up. With Elmer's glue, secure about 1½" of each muslin strip to a stile in an alternate pattern with about ¹⁄₁₆" separation between strips. Check for spilt glue which would prevent separation. Let dry. Turning panels over, pull the strips up through the joints and secure as shown. Scene paint will mask the flaps. Paint into each joint in both positions.

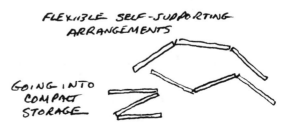

4' x 8' Veneer Panels
(interclamped)
for Interior Scenes

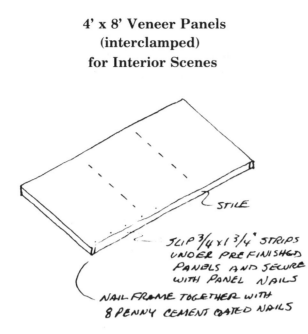

STILE

SLIP 3/4 x 1 3/4" STRIPS UNDER PREFINISHED PANELS AND SECURE WITH PANEL NAILS

NAIL FRAME TOGETHER WITH 8 PENNY CEMENT COATED NAILS

Note that the battens are set at right angles to the panel as shown on page 66 rather than being laid flat as in conventional scenic framing. Shown below is clamping for a straight-run wall, also clamping strip for an "on-edge" brace jack.

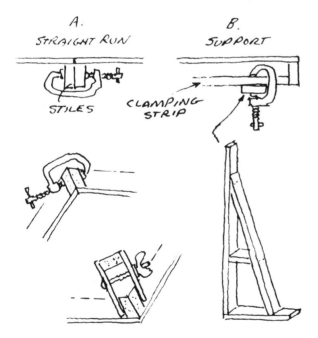

A.
STRAIGHT RUN

B.
SUPPORT

STILES

CLAMPING STRIP

The only effective way of turning corners with panels built with framing member on edge is by mitering. Rip the stiles with angled blade and use the miter gauge for cutting the rails. For certain turns, C-clamps will not fit in, so special "clothes-pin" clamps must be made, or use bolts through oversize holes.

For wallpapering and painting, use Upson Board panels.

Panels can be extended in height by lengthening the stiles and doubling the top rails for panel joints. Also molding, cornice, etc., can be clamped on. Here the door itself is made from the removed panel by adding rails, stiles and muntins from custom-ripped pieces of ¾" shelving.

4' x 8' Upson Board Panels
for Exteriors of Huts, Etc.

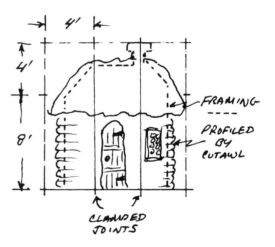

4'

4'

8'

FRAMING

PROFILED BY CUTAWL

CLAMPED JOINTS

Shown above is an interclamped forest hut. Two 8' high brace jacks should be sufficient for support. Again, the door is made from the piece removed by the addition of flat framing, this time, to the rear.

Twofold Tree Framed on Edge

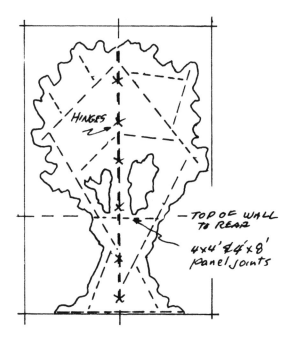

This tree was made from three ³⁄₁₆" 4' x 8' Upson Board sheets and framed on edge in order to be clamped to an adjacent garden wall itself framed in the fashion shown on page 74. However, the two tree parts were metal-hinged on face with a muslin dutchman strip placed over the vertical joint prior to painting. This concealed the crack and made for quick assembly.

The Roll Drop

The technician who finds this sort of scenery particularly useful will usually be performing in spaces where there are no fly lofts; however, roll drops can often be used to good advantage.

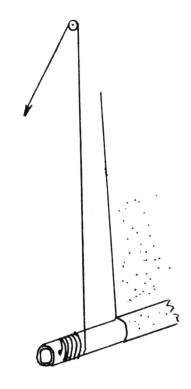

The above drawing shows the correct manner of rigging a roll drop, by which the roll is forced to "walk up" the drop. This action makes the drop support the roll and sagging is avoided. Note also that the drop should be tapered to maintain a proper tautness along the sides.

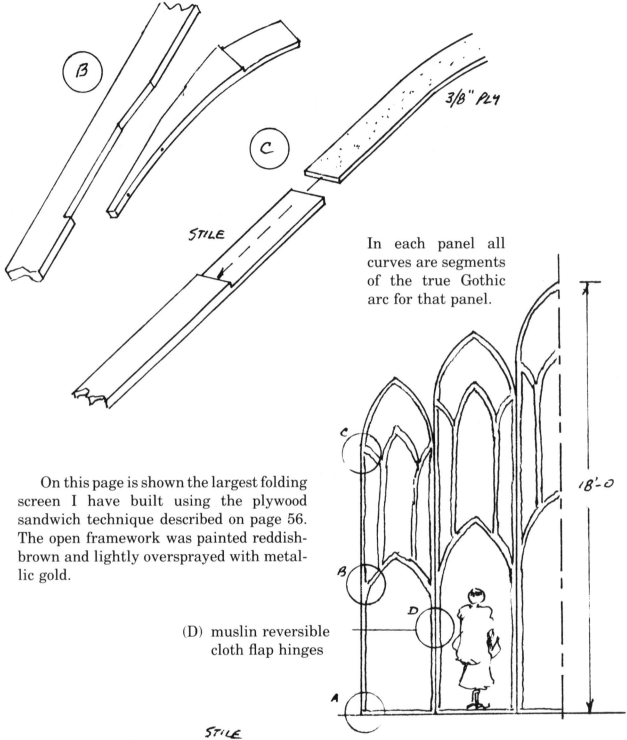

B

C

3/8" PLY

STILE

In each panel all curves are segments of the true Gothic arc for that panel.

On this page is shown the largest folding screen I have built using the plywood sandwich technique described on page 56. The open framework was painted reddish-brown and lightly oversprayed with metallic gold.

(D) muslin reversible cloth flap hinges

18'-0

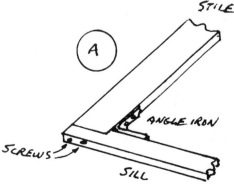

A

STILE

ANGLE IRON

SCREWS

SILL

All structural members with the exception of the sills measure ¾" x 2¼". The stiles, sill pieces and short arch haunch pieces are of Ponderosa pine. Once you pass into the true ⅜" ply sandwich, any shape can be mastered. Adequate structure is a matter of properly offsetting the joints. Overlapping pieces are glued and bradded.

For this fifth edition, I am stepping down as publisher and assigning the copyright to Meriwether Publishing Ltd. and Contemporary Drama Service, in the past one of my principal distributors, as well as the publishers of my other booklets, *Stage Lighting in the Boondocks, Small Stage Sets on Tour,* and *Stagecraft for Christmas and Easter Plays.* They will continue my practice of using exact-size reproductions of the sheets I have prepared myself, so that all graphics remain as drawn. This means that if I used a certain scale for a drawing, then the same scale can be used by the reader in order to determine measurements not given. All scaled drawings are so noted. On perspective sketches, pertinent measurements are shown. Since the third edition was published in 1976, certain techniques not shown previously have become very popular, and these are now included in a short supplement that will be found on pages 109 through 112.

**Now That *Self-Supporting Scenery*
Has Helped You Build Outstanding Sets,
You Will Need
These Other Theatrecraft Books
By James Hull Miller:**

STAGE LIGHTING
IN THE BOONDOCKS

by JAMES HULL MILLER

Self-Supporting Scenery has shown you that you needn't buy the expensive help of experts to have great freestanding scenery. But the mystique of stage lighting can be intimidating. You know good lighting is more than a few spotlights, yet you don't think your little theatre group can afford expensive lighting equipment. ***Stage Lighting in the Boondocks*** shows and tells how professional-quality lighting can be achieved within the limitations of school auditoriums, community theatres and churches. This workshop book is fully illustrated and has a section for reference notes. Author James Hull Miller covers everything from how much light you need, to the use of projected scenery, to how to approach diffusion lighting, power hookups and homemade equipment. Available at many bookstores or from Meriwether Publishing Ltd., P.O. Box 7710, Colorado Springs, Colorado 80933.

SMALL STAGE SETS ON TOUR

by JAMES HULL MILLER

Leading authority on portable stage sets, James Hull Miller discusses the design, construction and application of portable stage sets. Dozens of actual sets and how to build them are included. Also examines various types of theatres and other playing spaces encountered in traveling productions. There are chapters on folding and clamped sets, stagecraft in schools and churches, and small theatre designs. Miller recounts many of his backstage experiences and discusses the theory taught at his Arts Lab in Shreveport, LA. An indispensable resource for stage crews and theatre students. Available at many bookstores or from Meriwether Publishing Ltd., P.O. Box 7710, Colorado Springs, Colorado 80933.

ORDER FORM

MERIWETHER PUBLISHING LTD.
P.O. BOX 7710
COLORADO SPRINGS, CO 80933
TELEPHONE: (719) 594-4422

Please send me the following books:

_____**Self-Supporting Scenery #TT-B105** $10.95
by James Hull Miller
A scenic workbook for the open stage

_____**Stage Lighting in the Boondocks #TT-B141** $6.95
by James Hull Miller
A simplified guide to stage lighting

_____**Small Stage Sets on Tour #TT-B102** $9.95
by James Hull Miller
A practical guide to portable stage sets

_____**Original Audition Scenes for Actors #TT-B129** $9.95
by Garry Michael Kluger
A book of professional-level dialogs and monologs

_____**57 Original Auditions for Actors #TT-B181** $9.95
by Eddie Lawrence
A workbook of monologs for actors

_____**Theatre Games for Young Performers #TT-B188** $9.95
by Maria C. Novelly
Improvisations and exercises for developing acting skills

_____**Winning Monologs for Young Actors #TT-B127** $9.95
by Peg Kehret
Honest-to-life monologs for young actors

These and other fine Meriwether Publishing books are available at your local bookstore or direct from the publisher. Use the handy order form on this page.

I understand that I may return any book
for a full refund if not satisfied.

NAME: _____

ORGANIZATION NAME: _____

ADDRESS: _____

CITY: _____ STATE: _____ ZIP: _____

PHONE: _____

☐ **Check Enclosed**
☐ **Visa or Mastercard #** _____

                                                          Expiration
Signature: _____ *Date:* _____
               (required for Visa/Mastercard orders)

COLORADO RESIDENTS: Please add 3% sales tax.
SHIPPING: Include $1.50 for the first book and 50¢ for each additional book ordered.

☐ *Please send me a copy of your complete catalog of books and plays.*

ORDER FORM

MERIWETHER PUBLISHING LTD.
P.O. BOX 7710
COLORADO SPRINGS, CO 80933
TELEPHONE: (719) 594-4422

Please send me the following books:

_____**Self-Supporting Scenery #TT-B105**   **$10.95**
by James Hull Miller
A scenic workbook for the open stage

_____**Stage Lighting in the Boondocks #TT-B141**   **$6.95**
by James Hull Miller
A simplified guide to stage lighting

_____**Small Stage Sets on Tour #TT-B102**   **$9.95**
by James Hull Miller
A practical guide to portable stage sets

_____**Original Audition Scenes for Actors #TT-B129** **$9.95**
by Garry Michael Kluger
A book of professional-level dialogs and monologs

_____**57 Original Auditions for Actors #TT-B181**   **$9.95**
by Eddie Lawrence
A workbook of monologs for actors

_____**Theatre Games for Young Performers #TT-B188** **$9.95**
by Maria C. Novelly
Improvisations and exercises for developing acting skills

_____**Winning Monologs for Young Actors #TT-B127** **$9.95**
by Peg Kehret
Honest-to-life monologs for young actors

**These and other fine Meriwether Publishing books are available at
your local bookstore or direct from the publisher. Use the handy
order form on this page.**

*I understand that I may return any book
for a full refund if not satisfied.*

NAME: _____

ORGANIZATION NAME: _____

ADDRESS: _____

CITY: _____ STATE: _____ ZIP: _____

PHONE: _____

☐ **Check Enclosed**
☐ **Visa or Mastercard #** _____

*Signature:*_____ *Expiration
Date:*_____

(required for Visa/Mastercard orders)

COLORADO RESIDENTS: Please add 3% sales tax.
SHIPPING: Include $1.50 for the first book and 50¢ for each additional book ordered.

☐ *Please send me a copy of your complete catalog of books and plays.*

ORDER FORM

MERIWETHER PUBLISHING LTD.
P.O. BOX 7710
COLORADO SPRINGS, CO 80933
TELEPHONE: (719) 594-4422

Please send me the following books:

_____**Self-Supporting Scenery #TT-B105**　　　　**$10.95**
by James Hull Miller
A scenic workbook for the open stage

_____**Stage Lighting in the Boondocks #TT-B141**　　**$6.95**
by James Hull Miller
A simplified guide to stage lighting

_____**Small Stage Sets on Tour #TT-B102**　　　　**$9.95**
by James Hull Miller
A practical guide to portable stage sets

_____**Original Audition Scenes for Actors #TT-B129**　**$9.95**
by Garry Michael Kluger
A book of professional-level dialogs and monologs

_____**57 Original Auditions for Actors #TT-B181**　　**$9.95**
by Eddie Lawrence
A workbook of monologs for actors

_____**Theatre Games for Young Performers #TT-B188**　**$9.95**
by Maria C. Novelly
Improvisations and exercises for developing acting skills

_____**Winning Monologs for Young Actors #TT-B127**　**$9.95**
by Peg Kehret
Honest-to-life monologs for young actors

These and other fine Meriwether Publishing books are available at your local bookstore or direct from the publisher. Use the handy order form on this page.

I understand that I may return any book
for a full refund if not satisfied.

NAME: _____

ORGANIZATION NAME: _____

ADDRESS: _____

CITY: _____ STATE: _____ ZIP: _____

PHONE: _____

☐ **Check Enclosed**
☐ **Visa or Mastercard #** _____

　　　　　　　　　　　　　　　　　　Expiration
*Signature:*_____ *Date:*_____
　　　　(required for Visa/Mastercard orders)

COLORADO RESIDENTS: Please add 3% sales tax.
SHIPPING: Include $1.50 for the first book and 50¢ for each additional book ordered.

☐ *Please send me a copy of your complete catalog of books and plays.*